To Penelope
My partner in life and travel.

THE GRA

ND TOUR

TASCHEN

HONG KONG KÖLN LONDON LOS ANGELES MADRID PARIS TOKYO

Front cover:
Agra, Taj Mahal, 1631-1657
Architect: Isa Khan

Back cover:
Sydney, Opera House, 1957-1973
Architect: Jørn Utzon

To stay informed about upcoming
TASCHEN titles, please request our
magazine at www.taschen.com/magazine
or write to TASCHEN America,
6671 Sunset Boulevard, Suite 1508,
USA-Los Angeles, CA 90028,
contact-us@taschen.com,
Fax: +1-323-463.4442. We will be
happy to send you a free copy of our
magazine which is filled with information
about all of our books.

Designed by Massimo Vignelli
Translation by Latido, Bremen

Printed in China
ISBN 978-3-8228-3780-1

Contents

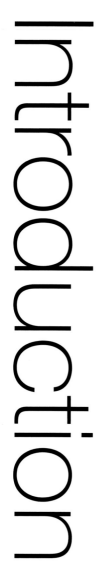

Introduction

This book aims to portray the peak achievements in architecture and the built environment that I have seen, all around the globe. The photos were taken by me over a period in excess of 50 years and show in juxtaposition the work of 3000 BC, up to the latest buildings of our own time. My predisposition to travel started involuntarily at the age of 15 in my native Vienna, which I left following the Anschluss in 1938. After a 10 year circuitous Odyssey from internment in England and Canada to studies there and the USA, to work in Brazil, I finally settled in Australia and commenced practice of architecture in 1948.

After some years, circumnavigation of the globe started with ever increasing frequency - to experience the most celebrated ancient and current architecture in Europe, Asia and America.

With frequent stops in Rome to consult with the engineer Pier Luigi Nervi on my concrete structures, I first experienced the impact of historic architecture in any depth. Developing what I call a passive appreciation and respect for the great building achievements of the past - I saw this as a simultaneous active love and dedication to developing an appropriate architecture, expressive of the artistic and technological impacts in building today. One can appreciate traditional architecture in relation to its period, the given circumstances of man's artistic aspirations, technical means and the social-political conditions of the time, as against the involved, active enthusiasm evoked by the masterpieces of the time in which one builds.

The ease and speed of jet travel opened up the world in the 1960s. The frequent visits to Rome were extended later involving trips to my buildings during construction in Paris, Mexico, Hong Kong and recently in my hometown of Vienna. In addition, teaching and lecturing in many countries amplified this routine to long distance flying 3 and 4 times a year, always with time for photography, recording the delight I felt seeing township environments and the icon buildings of all eras.

© Photo: Penelope Seidler

he extensive assembly of images aims to
be of international interest equally to the lay
public, architects, students of architecture
and historians, in the hope that they will be
encouraged to travel and seek out what I
feel to be much of the finest man has built
in our time and throughout recorded
history.
My photographer brother, Marcell (1919-
1977) gave me simple advice when I
started to record architectural sites "Only
use Leica cameras and Kodachrome film,
which is archival". I have adhered to this in
making all images in this book, some over
50 years ago.

Egypt

Egypt's antiquity has always stood out as unique in comparison to other cultures anywhere on the globe. What makes it so special are the works handed down to us, their gargantuan size, built millennia ago of solid stone; the pyramids, obelisks, temples, sculptures and artworks. It seems inconceivable to visualise how these enormous works, such as 250 ton stone obelisks, were physically brought into existence, extracted and erected, with the minimal technical means available, 5,000 years ago.

Spread along the fertile Nile River Valley, these great structures are spaced on both sides of the river. It was all developed by people with the longest lasting stable civilisation in antiquity.

The autocratic kings, who were worshipped as divine royalty, had huge works built as visible memorials, such as burial chambers contained in the great pyramids or colossal statues of their images. They left evidence of the enrichment in their lives through luxury articles and solid gold masks found in their tombs.

As an outstanding example, the God-King, Pharaoh Ramesses II, built the Temple to the God Amun at Karnak, with closely spaced sandstone columns some 25 m high and 3 m in diameter. The capitals are of Lotus form, covered with incised figures and hieroglyphics in the Hypostyle Hall, which is lit from above through clerestory openings. The surfaces of depository limestone or sandstone walls and columns have inevitably deteriorated and fretted away with time. The ancient Egyptians must have been well aware of this because when it came to sculpturing the images of their Gods, such as the Falcon Bird Horus, or the heads of Pharaohs, they used igneous stone such as solid granite.

Horus made of Aswan black granite has been standing exposed to the elements flanking the entrance of the Temple at Edfu for the last 3,500 years. It is in perfect condition, with edges sharp and features undisturbed. Whenever today's salesmen of new technology materials claim that their products will stand the test of time, I prefer

believe in the irrevocable evidence
offered by Horus in choosing exterior
materials for my buildings.
The form language used by the ancient
Egyptians in their structures is minimal.
The silhouettes read distinctively and
powerfully even from a distance. It is only
when approaching that one becomes
aware of the human figures and hieroglyphics incised in them, which gives
richness to the geometric forms. The
characteristic outwardly tapered Temple
walls shows evidence of an intuitive response to the need for lateral structural
stability and resistance to earthquakes.
The benign frost-free climate of Egypt
contributes to the remarkable condition
in which these structures have survived
for millennia.
With the construction of the Aswan high
dam in the 1960s, numerous ancient
monuments and temples were threatened
with inundation. Under the initiative of
UNESCO, some of them were saved
by being moved and reconstructed on
higher ground. The most dramatic of these
raisings were the Abu Simbel Colossal
sculptures of Ramesses II, which were
rebuilt against an artificially constructed
mountain with a final appearance identical
to the original.

1

1 Karnak, temple of Amun, 1550 BC

Gizeh, Pyramids of Cheops, 2250 BC
Builder: Cheops
The very icons of ancient Egypt, these giant animal sculptures stand in a sandy desert area near Cairo. The largest is 146,6 m high on a square base of 230 m, built of solid limestone blocks weighing some 2 tons each. The pyramid contains the King's, and below it, the Queen's burial chambers near its centre, reached by an internal sloping grand gallery, made of granite. Originally, the pyramids were covered in finely finished limestone with the peak reputed to have been covered in gold. All of this, however, was pillaged over the centuries.

Philae, Temple of Isis, 330 BC
Rebuilt on high ground to avoid dam inundation.

Edfu, Temple of Horus, 237-57 BC
The great Pylon-Portico has the characteristically tapered profile of a number of temples, which gives lateral stability to the 30 m high structure. A beautifully proportioned entrance is topped by a stone being element and opens onto an internal colonnaded court leading to the inner sanctum of the temple.

3

4

5 Sakkara, 3000 BC
Entrance into a palace court with beautifully proportioned opening and recesses in the masonry surface.

6 Karnak, Temple of Amun
Incised figures and hieroglyphics on a limestone wall.

7 Karnak, Temple of Amun
Entry into the Hypostyle Hall flanked by huge granite figures.

8 Karnak, Temple of Amun, 1550 BC
Hypostyle Hall with closely spaced huge columns, incised with figures and hieroglyphics.

5

6

9

10

9 Temple at Edfu, 237-57 BC

10 Luxor Temple
Head of Ramesses II.

11 Edfu, 237-57 BC
Granite figure of Horus at the entry to the Temple at Edfu.

12 Luxor Temple
Entry of Temple with seated figures and obelisk. The missing right side obelisk was taken to France in the 19th Century and erected on the Place de la Concorde (see France photo 45).

13 Philae, Temple of Isis, 330 BC
The Temple was raised and rebuilt faithfully on a high ground island prior to the flooding of the Aswan Dam. The symmetrical portico structure is reminiscent of other Temples, but visual enticement is created in the opposing irregular spatial disposition of the arcaded forecourt wings. Beautiful, everchanging spaces result as one walks through the complex.

1

2

14, 17 Nubia, Abu Simbel
The raised and rebuilt giant rock hewn sculptures of Ramesses II.

15 Nubia, Kalabsha Temple
The rebuilt Temple on high ground is only reachable by water.

16 Esna, Chnum-Temple
The Temple stands in a town and is surrounded by buildings. It is smaller than others with a colonnade enclosed by screen walls.

18 Gizeh, The Sphinx, 2500 BC
Damaged over centuries, it still represents an unforgettable image of a human head with an animal's body.

19 Thebes, Temple of Queen Hatshepsut, 1550 BC
Architect: Senenmut
The setting of this terraced mortuary temple is spectacular. Rising from the Nile Valley it is approached by ramps to 3 levels toward the base of dramatic high rock cliffs. Double colonnades surround walled courts with fine incised relief sculptures.

14

15

16

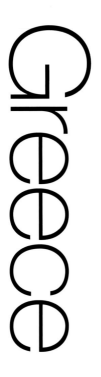

Greece

The rich legacy of ancient Greece between 500-300 BC formed the fountainhead of western civilisation; in the arts, in literature, skills of government, but especially in the influence of its refined architecture. The design of temple buildings contained such subtle depth of aesthetic sensibility as to become the prototypes of important buildings and monuments for the next 2,500 years. This heritage can rightfully be called "International Style" as against that term often used erroneously to describe 20th Century architecture, which changes constantly and is not a style.

Greek Architecture has been recorded and studied, particularly the optical refinements of temple facades, which were repeated for centuries on important buildings throughout most of the civilised world. The finest celebrated ancient examples are the sanctuary buildings on the Acropolis in Athens. They contain the visual adjustments devised to combat optical illusions and achieve a "corrected" view of reality for the onlooker. Marble column shafts were tapered toward the top to appear straighter and more graceful to the eye. Building bases were convex in the centre to look more horizontal and the spacing of portico end columns was made closer so as to appear more equal with the adjoining group, etc.

Column designs followed one of three main "Orders", the simplest being Doric, with fluted sharp arrised grooves, Ionic having voluted scroll capitals and Corinthian sculptured in the form of Acanthus leaves. Our eyes are fully attuned to seeing these ubiquitous Greek forms on buildings, which have been a prescribed style in certain periods of history. Construction of such buildings is highly labour intensive and virtually impossible to replicate today, and yet many people still feel comfortable and relate to them in preference to much of the architecture of our own time.

In more recent centuries, the architecture and urban fabric on the multitude of Greek Islands developed from the use of arches and domes especially in the celebrated steep hillside towns of Mykonos and Santorini.

1

1 Erectheion, 421-406 BC
Supporting Caryatid statue of a young
maiden, Erectheum, Athens.

2

3

2 Athens, Parthenon, 440 BC
Architects: Ictinus and Callicrates
The Parthenon temple of Athena,
considered the most perfect of classic
buildings in antiquity.

3 Athens, Erectheion, 421-406 BC
Architect: Mnesicles
An irregular building on the Acropolis with
an attached porch supported by Caryatids,
sculpted figures of young maidens instead
of columns.

4 Athens, Propylaea, 437-432 BC
The entrance portico to the Acropolis.

5 Athens, Acropolis
Built on a platformed mountain.

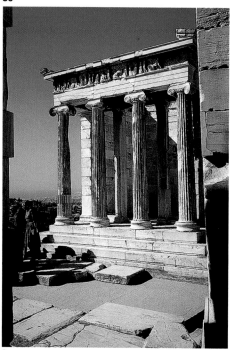

6

7

8

Athens, Temple of Athena, Nike
pteros, 427-424 BC
Architect: Callicrates
The small structure defies regularity by
being placed at an angle, resulting in a
dynamic spatial relationship with the
adjacent Propylaea.

Sounion, Temple of Poseidon, 440 BC
Built on a dramatic promontory east of
Athens overlooking the Aegean Sea.

Delphi, Amphitheatre
As many other Greek theatres, the semi-
circular seating is built into the natural slope
of the land and overlooks the splendid
mountain setting.

Delphi
The circular temple structure at the bottom
of a sloping site.

9

Italy

If there is one country and its people that have contributed most to western civilisation's man-made world continuously for the last 2000 years, it must surely be Italy. Starting with the vast Roman Empire, its colonising tentacles reaching most of Europe, there are the daring engineering structures: the architectural form language was inherited from the ancient Greeks, but the application into huge structures bears testimony to the Romans' intuitive engineering skills. These survive, mostly intact, to this day. The Romans were not inventors of the supporting arch, but its extended use in vaults and intersecting barrel shapes and domes is theirs. Structures such as the Pantheon in Rome or the impressive aqueducts they built, the Pont du Gard in France and at Segovia in Spain, the huge public baths, stadia and theatres, boggle the mind today, just to think that they were based on experiment. empirical knowledge without the mathematical systems of analysis that we know today.

In the Middle Ages, Italian towns grew not with a clear devised plan, but an organic assembly of tightly packed environments with narrow streets that burst open into most delightful public plazas that are the joy of inhabitants and of the envying hoard of tourists that frequent and travel through Italy, it seems continuously. After about the first Millennium, Italy was the cradle of Romanesque architecture, which spread throughout Europe, much of it extending the structural daring with mini-mal visual elaboration.

Borne out of this, starting around the 17th Century, was the Baroque era. It is my view that it is one of the architectural peak periods in western civilisation. The structur scheme of domed support was refined int spatially complex and daring backgrounds for the visual exuberance of painting and sculpture that adorn the period's celebrate works. My favourite is Borromini and his masterful Quattro Fontane and St. Ivo church interiors that combined a structura virtuosity achieved with geometrically mini-mal means in contrast to his exuberant riv

rnini, best known for his brilliant sculp-
es and elaborate fountains which are
ted throughout Rome – or Guarini's
ldings in Turin. It is still Borromini's
uctural inventions that have most to
/ to us to this day in that they show
hed interiors whose rib elements narrow
d deepen toward the top of domes,
cognising intuitively that greater stiffness
needed there. This is confirmed by
day's method of structural analysis.
wever, the mode of the Baroque era,
de from structural innovation, were its
corative embellishments which were
dearing at that time and have never
ased to fascinate and delight the visitor,
ch as Pozzo's magnificent frescos in
Ignacio. He remained in demand beyond
y, as did the muralist Tiepolo. The period's
uctural inventiveness bore fruit, was
peated and extended by the great
gineer-architect Balthazar Neumann in
th Century Germany (see Germany
otos 6-8).
e late Pier Luigi Nervi, in our time, is
rromini's structural descendent. He
presents the highpoint of 20th Century
ogressive engineering. His structures are
t only mathematically and construction-
/ logical, but deeply satisfying aesthe-
ally in that the static laws of nature are
de evident and are given form without
y painterly or sculptural embellishments –
ch as in his Olympic Stadia structures
the 1960s.

1

1 Rome, Circular Temple of Portunus
1st Century AD, by the Tiber.

3

4

2-4 Paestum, Temple of Neptune, 500 BC
The early best preserved Greek Temples.
The Doric columns in the centre are heavier
than later ones and are in superimposed
two tiers.

**5 Pompeii, Patrician's House,
2nd Century AD**
Interior courtyard.

Rome, Colosseum, 70-82 AD
he most magnificent of many Roman
mphitheatres, accommodated 60,000
pectators in an amazing engineering feat
or its time.

Taormina Theatre
he originally Greek and later Roman
heatre overlooks the beautiful coast of
icily.

-10 Rome, The Pantheon, 118-126 AD
he circular building has the same diameter
nd height of about 50 m – an engineering
iumph built in successively diminishing
ngs of stone with an open oculus in the
entre.

7

8

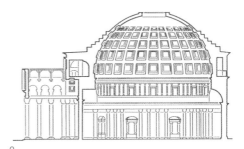

9

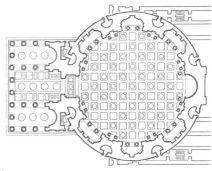

10

11

12

13

14

11 Pisa, Dom St. Maria Assunta and The Leaning Tower, 12th Century

12 Venice, St Mark's, 13th Century
Campanile rebuilt after collapse in 1902.

13 Siena, Palazzo Publico Tower, 1300
Overlooking the public plaza. Famous for its yearly horse race, the Palio.

14 Bologna, Brick Towers, 1100
Torre Asinelli and Garisenda.

15, 16 San Gimignano
The Tuscan hill town has high brick towers built by ruling families in the 10th and 11th Century. Their purpose is unclear and may have been for protection, storage, or simply rivalry between families to build high.

15

16

17-19 Mondavio

In the Marche area of eastern Italy are 15th Century fortified hill towns surrounded by high walls of brick. The "Rocca" defence towers are of extraordinary geometric shapes corbelling outward at the top.

20 Senigallia

The fortifications on the Adriatic Coast.

17

18

21 Orvieto, Cathedral, 1290-1500
Architect: Arnolfo di Cambio
Has a quasi-Gothic façade decorated with colourful mosaics.

22 Rome, Tempietto, 1502
Architect: Donato Bramante
A High Renaissance small circular domed temple is built in the cloister of S. Pietro in Montorio.

23 Florence, S. Maria Novella, 1300
Architect: Leon Battista Alberti
The Renaissance façade of 1460.

24 Mantua, S. Andrea, 1470-76
Architect: Leon Battista Alberti
The deeply recessed arched entry is one of the earliest Renaissance structures.

25 Venice, S. Zaccaria, 1450
Has a deeply moulded façade with beautiful arched roof forms.

26 Venice, Scuola di San Marco, 1490
Highlights of the arched elements of the façade are on either side of the entrance portals. Pictorial compositions in coloured marbles create perspective scenes, which appear to have a third dimension in depth.

21

22

23

24

25

26

27 Rome, Piazza del Popolo, 1670
Architect: C. Rainaldi
The central obelisk marks the converging point of three streets, flanked by two domed churches.

28 Rome, Piazza Navona, 1600s
Francesco Borromini's concave façade of the Sant' Agnese Church.

29 Florence, Ponte Veccio, 1345

30 Florence, Pitti Palace, 1460

31 Siena, 12th Century
Medieval tight network of narrow streets.

32 Siena Piazza del Campo, 14th Cent.
The open Campo, focus of the city.

33 Stra, Palace Pisani, 18th Century
The theatrical façade is merely a stable.

34 Venice, St Marks Square
The grandest urban space in Europe.

35 Rome, Piazza del Campidoglio, 1538
Architect: Michelangelo
The three buildings defining the trapezoidal plaza are placed apart to defy perspective and appear parallel.

36 Florence, Pazzi Chapel, 1429-61
Architect: Filippo Brunelleschi

37 Lucca
The oval-shaped central space follows the form of an ancient Roman amphitheatre.

38 Vigevano, 1492
Attributed to Donato Bramante. The painted facades reputed to be by Leonardo da Vinci.

39 Caserta, Royal Palace, 1752
Architect: Luigi Vanvitelli
The grand staircase in the octagonal vestibule creates multiple vistas in several directions.

40 Turin, San Lorenzo, 1668-87
Architect: Guarino Guarini
Based on octagonal geometrics the plan ends in a top-lit dome supported by eight interlocking ribs.

42

41 Venice, Santa Maria della Salute, 1630
Architect: Baldassare Longhena

42 Venice, Ca' d'Oro, 1430
Architects: Giovanni & Bartolommeo Buon

43

44

45

43 Maser, Villa Barbaro, 1550
Architect: Andrea Palladio
A combined country house with farm buildings.

44 Maser, Villa Barbaro, 1550
Architect: Andrea Palladio
Interior. The central wing has life-size wall frescos by Paolo Veronese.

45 Vicenza, Basilica, 1549
Architect: Andrea Palladio
The façade with the typical "Palladian" motive of Serliana openings of arches and columns.

46 Fanzolo, Villa Emo, 1565
Architect: Andrea Palladio
As with Villa Barbaro, a combined residence with arcaded access wings.

47 Urbino, 1450
The fortress-like palace of the Duke Federico da Montefeltro dominates the dramatic walled hill town.

48

48 Rome, St Peter's Piazza, 1656-1667
Architect: Gian Lorenzo Bernini
An appropriate setting for large crowds of pilgrims enclosed by huge semi-circular colonnades scaled to relate to the façade of St Peter's.

49 Gian Lorenzo Bernini, 1598-1680

50 Rome, St Peter's
Detail of the encircling colonnade's columns

51 Rome, St Peter's Basilica, 16th and 17th Century
Designed successively by a number of Architects, Donato Bramante, Michelangelo and Carlo Maderno. The focus of the enormous interior is Bernini's Baldachino supported by twisted bronze columns (looted from the Pantheon) under the great dome.

52 Rome, St Peter's Basilica, Plan

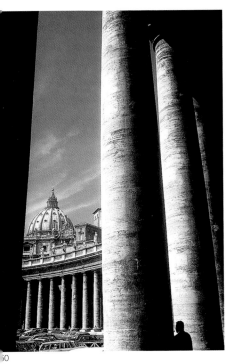

50

51

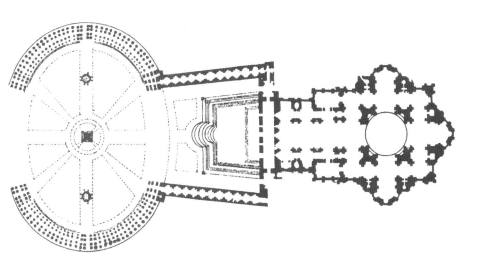

52

54

53 Rome, Piazza Navona "Four Rivers" Fountain, 1648-51
Architect: Gian Lorenzo Bernini
The fountain is fed by water from restored ancient aqueducts. It is placed in front of St Agnese, the concave fronted Church built by his architectural rival, Borromini.

54 Rome, The Chapel in the Collegio di Propaganda Fide, 1660
Architect: Francesco Borromini
The interlocking ceiling ribs emanating from the four corners of the hall indicate an early awareness of structural forces (see page 70).

55

55, 56, 58 Rome, S. Carlo alle Quattro Fontane, 1638-41

Architect: Francesco Borromini
Even though small in scale, this Church is a most celebrated masterpiece of early Baroque architecture. Its pulsating, undulating façade is unique for its period. It is based on clear geometric themes of related circles and ellipses, which are carried to the interior, and displays an intuitive response to structural forces.

The interior of the dome is composed of three geometric coffer forms, said to be symbolic of the Trinity. They diminish in size toward the top, thereby increasing the apparent height of the dome in perspective. In addition, the closer spacing of the ribs at the top gives the structure increased stiffness to resist the bending forces where they are greatest.

This building represents a rare simultaneous architectural solution to symbolic requirements, geometric-structural needs and aesthetic fulfilment of the totality.

57 Francesco Borromini, 1599-1667

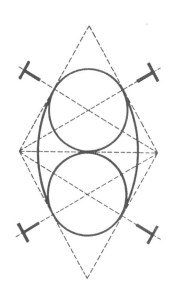

56

57

60

59-61 Rome, S. Ivo alla Sapienza, 1642-50
Architect: Francesco Borromini
The plan forms a six pointed star, with each 'point' replaced by alternating convex and concave curves. These are carried up to the base of the dome. The geometry changes and transforms toward the top into a circular oculus, which supports the lantern.

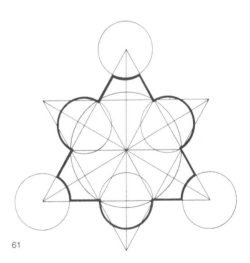

61

62, 63 Rome, S. Maria Della Pace, 1656-57
Architect: Pietro da Cortona
The projecting form of the Church increases the apparent size of the small surrounding urban square. Opposing convex and concave quadrant shaped curves both horizontally and vertically give the Church and Square a dynamic image.

64 Rome, Collegio di Propaganda Fide, 1660
Architect: Francesco Borromini
The concave-convex entrance façade.

65 Rome, S. Ignacio Church, 1691
Fresco by Fra Andrea Pozzo
The huge illusionary painting creates the perspective impression of great height.

66 Rome, Piazza S. Ignacio, 1727
Architect: Filippo Raguzzini
The oval shape of the stage setting like plaza is created by the concave facades of surrounding buildings.

62

63

9

0

67 Como, Casa del Fascio, 1936
Architect: Giuseppi Terragni
A pure and minimalistic example of Italian modern architecture, with a beautifully proportioned façade and spatial interiors.

68, 70 Bologna, L'Esprit Nouveau Pavilion
Architect: Le Corbusier
Reconstructed by the City of Bologna in a park, the exhibition building was first built for the 1925 Paris display. It contains a furnished maisonette apartment, the prototype for the 1947 Unité d'Habitation in Marseille. In an attached wing are top lit dioramas of Le Corbusier's concept drawings for his ideal city "Ville Radiense".

69 Rome, Railway Station, 1950
The entrance hall is given great height by upwardly shaped concrete roof beams, which form a projecting portico on the exterior.

71

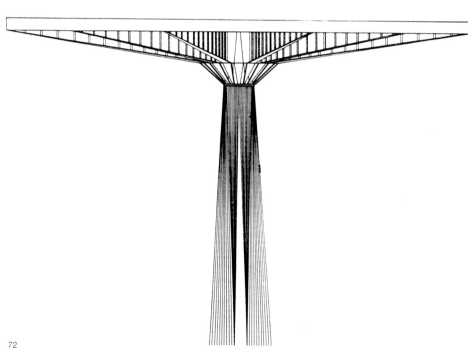

72

3

1, 72 Turin, Palace of Labour, 1960
Architect: Pier Luigi Nervi
The cantilevered steel roof beams are
supported by expressively tapered concrete
columns.

3 Mantua, Burgo Paper Mill, 1961
Architect: Pier Luigi Nervi
The 165 m span suspension structure is
carried by concrete trestles.

4 Pier Luigi Nervi, 1891-1979

74

5 Rome, Palazetto dello Sport, 1957
Architect: Pier Luigi Nervi
This smaller of the two Olympic Stadia built
for the 1960 Games was constructed of
precast "ferro cement" pans, a system
invented by Nervi, to form interlocking
concrete ribs poured between them to
span large distances.
The building represents a rare fusion of
rational structure with a sculpturally
satisfying aesthetic result.

Germany

Germany lost many of its architectural treasures during World War II (such as through the senseless bombing of Dresden). However, great buildings and environments in country areas and small towns remain and have mostly been painstakingly restored. The highlights are medieval towns with half timber buildings and charming squares, but particularly the palaces and churches of the Baroque era. Many of these are centred in the south east of the country, which came to be called "Pfaffenwinkel" (Parsons' corner), such as the churches Wies, Ettal, Ottobeuren, etc.

The work of the 18th Century architect Balthasar Neumann (originally a military engineer), is especially known for his pilgrimage church of Vierzehnheiligen (Fourteen Saints). It is a splendid Rococo building with interlocking twisted profile ribs supporting the wide masonry roof vaults. After a mid-19th Century fire in the timber roof, the structure was found to contain embedded iron bars in the stone and concrete vaults and ribs. I believe this to be the earliest and intuitive use of the principle of "reinforced concrete". The white ceiling and its exuberantly colourful frescoes remained intact after the fire.

Germany's unique contribution to architecture dates from the pioneering developments of the 1920s and 30s which were centred in the establishment by Walter Gropius of the "Bauhaus" in Weimar 1919 and later in Dessau 1925. That teaching and experimental institution has had a continuing influence in architecture, industrial design and art throughout most of the world to this day.

The principles developed at the Bauhaus aimed to bring into unison considerations of practical need, advanced technology and the art of the time, to form a Total Work of Art (Gesamtkunstwerk). Its far reaching influence is to be seen throughout the civilised world. The resulting forms of design remain in perpetual flux. They will change with time, responding to altered needs, advances in technology and developments in art. The many celebrated 20th Century buildings in different countries

give evidence of the fact that Modern architecture cannot be called a "style" of fixed design characteristics.
The methodology developed at the German Bauhaus remains valid with the passage of time.

1

1 Ulm, Cathedral, 1377-1477
The Gothic ribbed vaulted nave.

2 Munich, Nymphenburg Palace, 1730
Architect: Joseph Effner
The summer palace in its park setting.

4

-5 Vierzehnheiligen (Fourteen Saints), 750

Architect: Balthasar Neumann
with the Monastery of Banz in the distance
by Johann L. Dientzenhofer). The pilgrimage
church is a supreme example of Rococo
architecture in Germany. The comparatively
quiet exterior bursts forth on the interior
into a brilliant assembly of frescoed oval
and elliptical vaults.

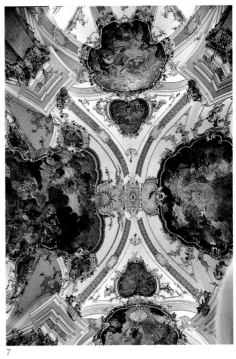

7

6-8 Vierzehnheiligen, 1750

Architect: Balthasar Neumann

The luminous quality of the interior results from the light admitted from large windows, reflected from a white structure in contrast to the colourful fresco paintings. The structural ingenuity of the building is evident at the "Vierung", the interaction of four vaults at their merging. The twisted surfaces of the supporting ribs are reminiscent of Pier Luigi Nervi's structures of 200 years later.

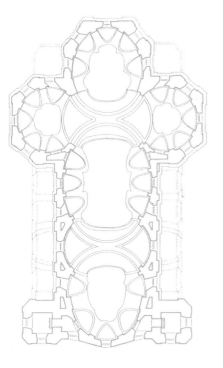

9
10
11
12

9 Neresheim, Monastery, 1745-64
Architect: Balthasar Neumann

10, 13 Munich, S. Johann Nepomuk, (Asamkirche), 1733-46
Architects: Asam Brothers
Built on a narrow city site, this Rococo Church is riotously decorated with undulating forms without any surface left plain.

11, 12, 15, 16 Würzburg, Residenz Palace, 1750
Architect: Balthasar Neumann (and others)
The Chapel and Emperor's halls with frescoes by the celebrated Venetian painter Giovanni Battista Tiepolo.
The grand staircase of 1735 with the ceiling fresco also by Tiepolo are the most satisfying and grandiose works of German Baroque.

14 Weltenburg, 1716-39
Architects: Asam Brothers
This Benedictine abbey is distinguished by indirect natural light from above, with the effect of intense artificial spotlighting falling on the focal altar and central sculpture of St. George and the dragon. The impact is that of a dramatic stage setting.

17 Neresheim, Monastery, 1745
Architect: Balthasar Neumann

18

19

20

18 Dresden, Opera, 1878
Architect: Gottfried Semper
Badly damaged during World War II, but
reconstructed faithfully.

19, 20 Dresden, Zwinger, 1710-28
Architect: Matthäus Daniel Pöppelmann
The suspended gilded crown dome over
the entrance to the complex across a
bridge.

21

21-23 Potsdam, Sanssouci, 1745
Architect: Georg Wenzeslaus von Knobelsdorff
Built as a retreat for Fredrick the Great, the approach is through a semi-circular colonnade into a long, one-storey pavilion with a sumptuously furnished domed oval hall. On the view side, a grand stair leads down to a large fountain flanked by terraced orangeries and vineyards.

2

3

24

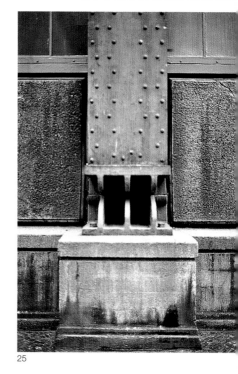

25

26

28

27

24, 25 Berlin, AEG Turbine Hall, 1908
Architect: Peter Behrens
A pioneering industrial steel structure with riveted exposed columns on pivoted supports.

26, 27 Alfeld, Faguswerke, 1911
Architect: Walter Gropius
A glass "curtain wall" building revolutionary for its time, covering the floors and structure, except for the expressed columns.

28 Walter Gropius, 1883-1969

29

29, 32 Dessau, Bauhaus, 1925
Architect: Walter Gropius
Not only did this building house an institute
developing a new approach to architecture,
industrial design and art, but it is a famous
example of architecture expressive in its
parts of diverse purposes.
The workshop wing is fully glazed for
maximum daylight. Classroom wings have
continuous horizontal ribbon windows; the
"Prellerhaus" students' studio and living
quarters have individual balconies, etc.

30

30, 31 Dessau, Bauhaus, 1925
Examples of innovative industrial design;
exposed and connected fluorescent tubes
on the ceiling in patterns recalling abstract
paintings of the time.
The tubular steel folding theatre seating
designed by Marcel Breuer.

31

2

33 Berlin, Gropiusstadt, 1963-73
Architect: Walter Gropius
A huge housing development in an open park setting with low, medium and high-rise structures.

34 Berlin, 1927
The residence of architect Erich Mendelsohn.

35 Berlin, Neue Nationalgalerie, 1968
Architect: Mies van der Rohe

36 Frankfurt, Museum für Moderne Kunst, 1987-90
Architect: Hans Hollein
The building takes on the shape of its triangular site. On the interior new concepts of spatial interplay dominate.

37, 38 Munich, Olympic Site, 1972
Architect: Frei Otto
A covering structure of plastic panels is suspended from metal poles. The huge hanging roof seems to deny conventional concepts of gravity.

39 Weil am Rhein, Vitra Design Museum, 1989
Architect: Frank Gehry
The unconventional geometry defying regular repetitive structure evolved from computer equipment to generate and produce any shape of structural elements. The large entrance sculpture depicting carpentry tools is by Claes Oldenburg.

40 Stuttgart, Weißenhof Siedlung, 1927
Architect: Le Corbusier
Duplex Housing in the influential Deutscher Werkbund Housing Display.

41-44 Bonn, Kunstmuseum, 1985-93
Architect: Axel Schultes
Its architecture maximises spatial effects by fusing areas horizontally and vertically.

33

34

35

36

7

38

9

40

1

42

3

44

France

The development of architecture in France reached many high points throughout history. From the ancient Roman province of Gallia, some daring engineering structures remain, such as the Pont du Gard, a 50 m high aqueduct built 2,000 years ago of unadorned three tier supporting stone arches.

The Romanesque era in the 11th and 12th Centuries produced unique churches and fortified towns. A peak was reached in the Gothic period when dramatic cathedrals with majestic stained glass windows were built higher and wider than any others in Europe; such as at Beauvais. The structural ingenuity achieving such huge enclosed spaces by means of thin stone piers stabilised by double flying buttresses is truly admirable.

The 16th Century saw elaborate fortified palatial chateaus built by the aristocracy in beautiful natural settings, often surrounded by water. The 17th Century was the era of sumptuous chateaus extended into man-made monumental formal gardens with axial vistas as far as the eye can see. One of the most brilliant is Vaux-le-Vicomte, which was built for a State Minister under Louis XIV, Nicolas Fouquet, who commissioned the architect Le Veau, the garden architect Le Notre and interiors by Lebrun. The King, invited to the extravagant house opening celebration became furious that one of his Ministers dared to outdo him with such a sumptuous establishment. He ordered the house closed, put Fouquet in prison and commandeered his team of designers to build him such a palace, only bigger and better. The result was Versailles. Bigger and more sumptuous it is, but not as exquisite aesthetically.

In prison, Fouquet was often visited by his architects, but never recovered from his misfortunes. He died 19 years later.

With the advent of the industrial revolution, the great rebuilding of Paris took place in the middle of the 19th Century under Napoleon III and his town planner, Haussmann. The grandeur of the Boulevards and axes of Paris, admired to this day, was made possible by the vision of this

owerful Emperor and his architect. Their
lans cut through the congested medieval
arts of the city to give it more light and
r, but also serve a strategic purpose of
lowing unhindered military movement to
uell citizen revolts. Following the techno-
gical and industrial advances made in
ngland, the combination of iron structures,
achines and the ambition to display the
ew means in the Paris world exhibition
1889, produced some remarkable build-
gs. The icons of the time at the end of
ie 19th Century were huge assemblies
cast iron elements, such as the Eiffel
ower. It took a long time to give true visual
xpression to the potential of the new
aterials. Initially, the vaulted forms of
aditional masonry architecture and even
ant decorations were imitated in iron. In
ie early years of the 20th Century the
ansient fashion of Art Nouveau used
ecorative curvilinear forms made of cast
on in stair railings and for entries to new
nderground stations of the Paris Metro.
ie most significant new development
r our own time took place about the end

1

1 Paris, Trocadero
View from the Eiffel Tower

World War I. Stimulated by the new art
the time such as the work of Cubist
ainters, architecture employed not only
novative technology and materials, but
sponded to the emerging new demands
n buildings expected to be satisfied in a
tional way.
eading in this, from the 1920s onward,
as the great architect, Le Corbusier. He
evoted his time to painting in the morning
d architecture in the afternoon. His pro-
c output in all related spheres, in paint-
gs, building, visionary town planning
chemes, and furniture, are without equal.
is impossible for an architect working
the 20th Century and today to claim
at he is not influenced in some way, by
e Corbusier's visions and executed work.
gether with Gropius, Mies van der Rohe
d Frank Lloyd Wright, France's Le
orbusier is the greatest of these recog-
sed "form givers" in architecture, whose
ork is beyond fashion and remains valid
actically and visually, to this day.

2

2 Nimes, Pont du Gard, 19 BC
A spectacular Roman aqueduct engineering
feat 50 m high. The supporting arch
structure remains unadorned to serve
purely its utilitarian purpose.

3 Poitiers, Notre-Dame-la-Grande, 1140
A Romanesque masterpiece with a
sculptured entrance façade, conical turrets
and dome.

**4 Paris, Notre-Dame Cathedral, started
1163**
The high nave is braced by double span
flying buttresses. Large circular transept
stained glass windows are held by thin
stone tracery.

5 Beauvais Cathedral 1247 started, completed in the 16th Century

At 50 m it is the highest and widest of Gothic Cathedrals, plagued by structural failures and rebuilding during the long construction period. Only the apse end remains, which is awe inspiring with high clerestory windows.

6 Vézelay, S. Madeleine, 1089-1206

Romanesque Church with a high unadorned two-tone semi-circular stone arched nave.

7, 8 Chartres Cathedral, 1220

The building with two unequal height towers is made famous by the magnificent predominantly blue stained glass windows.

9, 10 Paris, Sainte-Chapelle, 1240

Architect: Pierre de Montrevil
A small court chapel, but very high for its width, almost entirely of 15 m high stained glass. The vaulted ceiling is decorated bright blue.

5

6

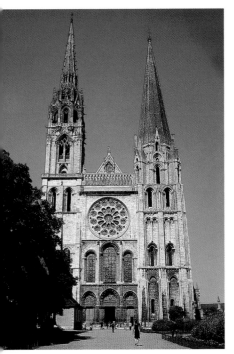

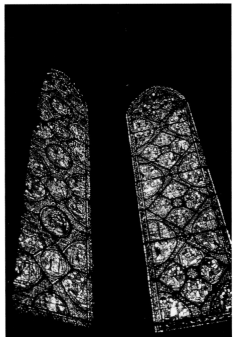

8

10

11, 13 Carcassonne
A fortified medieval town containing a
castle, churches and a theatre. Fallen into
disrepair it was restored in the 19th Century
by Architect Viollet-le-Duc.

12, 14 Albi Cathedral, 1280-1390
A fortress-like brick structure with projecting
round piers. Attached to its side entrance,
a finely ribbed Gothic portico was added
which creates a fascinating contrast to the
ponderous main building.

11

12

3

4

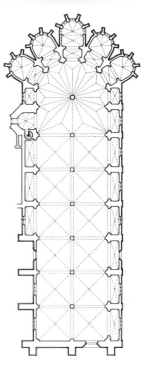

15   16

15, 16 Toulouse, Les Jacobins, 1260
The early Gothic rib-vaulted roof is
supported by a central row of columns,
which culminate in a beautiful palm-tree like
semi-circular apse end.

17 Vendome Cathedral, 1300
This small flamboyant Gothic structure has
flame-shaped window tracery and wide
span flying buttresses.

18 Amboise
Seen from the high platform surrounding
the chateau overlooking the Loire River. The
consistent roof slopes covered in grey slate
creates a serene, consistent townscape.

19

20

19 Rocamadour
Clinging dramatically to the cliffs of a river gorge, the stepped and ramped streets offer charming internal spaces and outward views of the Dordogne Valley.

20, 21 Saint-Cirq Lapopie
A charming country townscape with medieval timber framed and brick-infilled houses.

22 Grosbois Chateau, 1580
A typical formally planned steep roofed structure.

23, 24 Langeais Chateau, 1460
The interiors have exposed materials; masonry walls, timber ceilings and glazed tile floors. Tapestries lent warmth to the otherwise hard surfaced spaced.

25 Azay-le-Rideau Chateau, 1520
One of the most exquisite chateaus in the Valley of the Indre River. The nearest thing to a fairy tale castle is surrounded by water and superb forests.

26 Chenonceau, Chateau, 1540
Built across the river, this elegant building with long galleries overlooking the tranquil water has a long history of jealousies of different Kings, their wives and mistresses.

27 Vaux-le-Vicomte Chateau, 1660
Architects: Le Veau, Le Notre and Lebrun
The most elegant and grandiose of chateaus and formal gardens. Its owner, Fouquet, was put in jail for daring to outdo the King with such a sumptuous establishment.

28 Chambord, Chateau, start of construction 1590
Architect: Domenico da Cortona
Of all the 16th Century chateaus, this must be the most unbelievably bizarre, bristling with gables, pinnacles, domes and decorated chimneys surrounding a long turreted structure. Its ingenious central double spiral staircase allows a person walking up not to be seen by someone descending.

25

27

29

29 Valençay, Chateau, 1540
Set in an extensive property with a deer park surrounding the chateau, unusual corner domes give the building a distinctive silhouette.

30, 32 Chantilly, Chateau, 1560
Architect: Bullant
Set in a lake, every façade of the building is of different design and yet achieves cohesion of the whole.

31 Blois, Chateau, 1520-1630
Architect: Mansart
The distinctive element is the polygonal open staircase tower, which offers changing spatial through-views into the courtyard as one ascends.

33 d'Anet Chateau, 1550
Architect: Philibert de l'Orme
Has a fine curvilinear entrance staircase in one of the few remaining parts of the building.

34 Cheverny, Chateau, 1634
Architect: Boyer de Blois
Axially approached, the symmetrical building's flat façade achieves distinction from its varying height and shape roof forms. One of the most elegant chateaus in France.

35 Paris, Place des Vosges, 1605-12
Architect: Louis Metezeau
A fine urban square surrounded by arcaded individual residential buildings, each with its own roof. The two larger axial pavilions are reserved for the King and Queen.

34

35

118

36 Ménars Chateau, 1760
Architect: Ange-Jacques Gabriel
The formality of the approach is recalled in the artificially trimmed trees.

37, 38 Champs-sur-Seine, Chateau
A formal building with a seemingly endless axially landscaped park on the view side.

39, 41 Versailles Palace 1660
Architects: Le Veau and Mansart
Petit Trianon, 1760, Architect: Gabriel
The most immense palace building in Europe reflecting the total power of Louis XIV. The enormity of the complex is difficult to grasp as is the immense formal landscaped park and fountains surrounding it. Other than the Hall of Mirrors, it is a complex, less satisfying aesthetically than smaller palaces by the same architects.

40 Maisons–Lafitte Chateau, 1642-48
Architect: François Mansart
An urban grandiose chateau near Paris of majestic scale and great elegance.

36

37

38

39

42

43

42 Paris, The Invalides, 1678-91
Architect: Libéral Bruant
With a 200 metre long façade is one of Paris' landmarks. The building was used as a soldiers' hospital under Napoleon I who is buried in the domed structure at the rear.

43 Paris, Saint-Étienne-du-Mont, start of construction 1492
by Philibert de L'Orme
With its unique screen structure in front of the apse end, spanning between two spiral stone stairs.

44 Paris, Eiffel Tower, 1889
Built for the universal exhibition, this daringly light steel structure has become the iconic landmark of Paris. It is symbolic of new methods of construction.

45 Paris, Place de la Concorde, 1750
Architect: Ange-Jacques Gabriel
This axially placed open urban space, the very centre of Paris, is marked by a granite Egyptian obelisk (see Egypt photo 12 for its pair).

46

47

46 Monte Carlo, Casino, 1863
Architect: Charles Garnier
Symbolic of luxurious buildings in Europe's gambling capital.

47 Paris, Opera House, 1861-74
Architect: Charles Garnier
Built in the final phase of romantic 19th Century architecture, it is the ultimate example of decorative classicism.
A sumptuously curved grand staircase joins the high spaces of the foyer. A monument to the architect is built along one exterior façade.

48, 49 Paris, Rue de Rivoli, 1840
Architects: Percier & Fontaine
This one-sided arcaded straight line row of buildings was first built by Napoleon I. Overlooking the Tuileries Gardens, it forms a monumental element in the planning of Paris.

**0 Menier Chocolate Works, Noisiel-
ur-Marne, 1879**
rchitect: Jules Saulnier
he first iron skeleton supported building
ith non-structural brick infill exterior walls.

**1 Paris, Library Sainte-Geneviève,
850**
rchitect: Henri Labrouste
n early expressive wrought and cast iron
aulted structure.

2 Paris, National Library, 1860
rchitect: Henri Labrouste
he spherical roof vaults, each with a sky-
ght, are supported by slim cast iron
olumns.

3 Paris, Ave Rapp Apartments, 1900
rchitect: Jules Lavirotte
typical art nouveau decorated exterior.

51

52

53

54

55

54, 57 Paris, Grand Palais, 1897-1900
Architect: Frantz Jourdain
The huge exhibition building supports
its glass dome roof with iron ribs using
inappropriate forms of traditional
masonry vaults.

55, 58, 59 Paris, Métropolitain Stations, 1900
Architect: Hector Guimard
Art Nouveau cast iron and glass structures
in organic decorative forms.

56 Paris, Rue Reaumur, 1900
Architect: Georges Chedanne
An early example of exposed steel framed
construction.

58

59

60

60, 61 Villa Garches, 1927
Architect: Le Corbusier
This luxurious house built for the famous
Stein family in the country near Paris
represents an important milestone in Le
Corbusier's work. It demonstrates the clear
separation of structure and infill, enabling
spaces to be free and open aesthetically,
both horizontally and vertically. This seminal
building has influenced architecture to this
day.

62-64 Paris, Villa La Roche-Jeanneret, 1923
Architect: Le Corbusier
An early duplex residence with interiors of
spatial complexity. The building now houses
the Le Corbusier Foundation.

65-66 Paris, Apartments, 1933
Architect: Le Corbusier
The glass and glass blocks curtain wall
building houses the architect's two-storey
penthouse and landscaped roof terrace.

67 Paris, Swiss Students Pavilion, University of Paris, 1930
Architect: Le Corbusier
Supported on central concrete pylons and
a steel superstructure, all students' rooms
have straight south facing glass walls,
contrasted by the sculptural forms of the
common room and vertical core.

68-71 Poissy, Villa Savoie, 1929
Architect: Le Corbusier
The iconic best known of the architect's
houses, is built on a large property outside
of Paris. The dramatic spatial fusion of
the upper level hollow centre with access
ramps and spiral stairs make this a
supreme example of the fusion of art
and architecture.

65

66

67

72 Paris, Salvation Army Refuge, 1929
Architect: Le Corbusier
An early framed structure and the first totally sealed air conditioned glass curtain wall building. The façade was altered after World War II.

73, 75 Marseille, L'Unité d'habitation 1947
Architect: Le Corbusier
The tower contains split-level apartments with a central shopping floor, a roof top kindergarten and communal facilities.

72

74 Le Corbusier 1887-1965

76-83 The Chapel at Ronchamp, 1950
Architect: Le Corbusier
This represents a unique sculptural departure from conventional modern architecture. The awe-inspiring curvilinear interior receives daylight from various apertures in side-walls and top light through attached tower structures. The huge pivoted entrance is covered with a colourful metal mural by the architect.

73

84, 85, 87 Paris, Brazilian Students' Pavilion, University of Paris, 1957
Architect: Le Corbusier
Each students' room faces a sunny balcony. The ground level adjuncts contain communal facilities and a separate wing of the Director's residence.

74

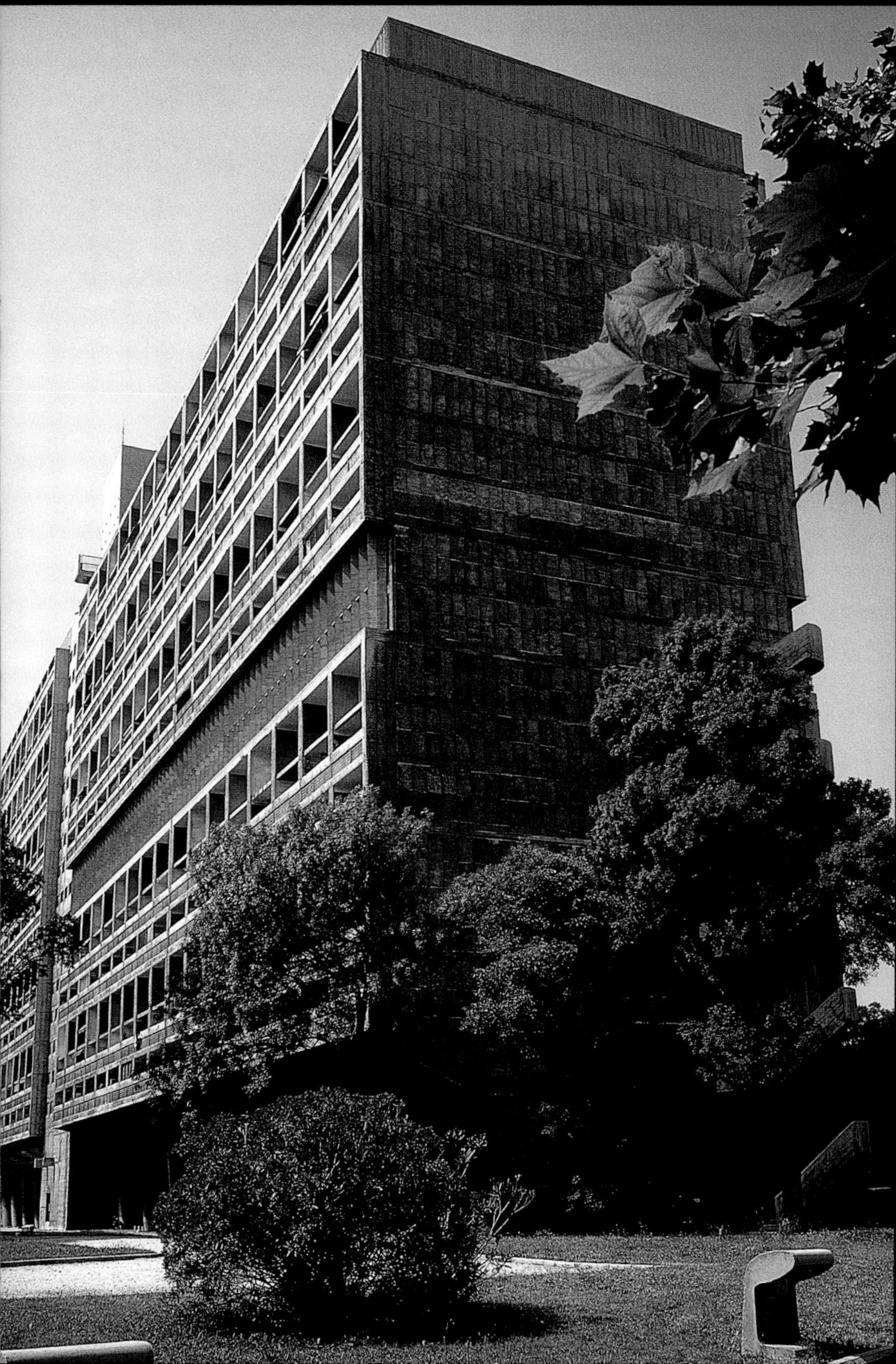

76

77

78

79

80

86, 89-93 Convent of La Tourette, 1960
Architect: Le Corbusier
The open central courtyard is surrounded
by monks' rooms and communal facilities.
A top lit colourful chapel is adjacent to the
large church hall.

88 Paris, Duplex Jaoul Residence, 1956
Architect: Le Corbusier
The brick walls and off form concrete
Catalan vault structure's colourful interiors
remain unadorned.

94 Paris, The Pyramid in the Louvre 1981
Architect: Ieoh Ming Pei
The ephemeral transparent pyramid is
placed over the large entry space leading
down to the wings of the museum.

84

85

87

86

88

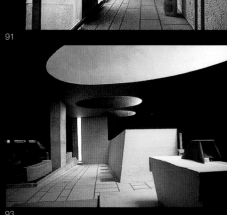

United Kingdom

The peak achievement in historic English architecture is the great number of churches and cathedrals built in the Gothic era. Medieval villages still maintain their unique charm, as does the elegant restraint of the numerous country manors and universities built in the Renaissance and Baroque periods.

Rather than the grandiose formal axes of French urban developments, the architecture of English cities is on a smaller scale and gains from the interaction of diverse styles side-by-side, often built centuries apart.

The building of continuous long terrace house developments in the 18th and 19th Century gives its own grandeur on smaller scale to towns, culminating in the superb urban planning of cities like Bath, which has been meticulously maintained and remains as valid today as it was 250 years ago.

The Industrial Revolution, technological and scientific advances were dramatic in the 19th Century, which brought a new vision to English architecture. Building upon 18th Century inventions of the use of iron in construction, the (later) glass and iron exhibition buildings influenced the rest of Europe.

The development of modern architecture aesthetically did not gain a foothold in England until just before World War II, with only a few distinguished buildings remaining. Although leaders of the modern movement in Europe (Gropius, Breuer, Mendelsohn, etc) came to England in the 1930s, having left Germany due to its emerging fascism, they were not welcomed professionally and left to teach and practice successfully in the USA.

Advances in building technology took a leap forward after the war with the work of outstandingly inventive architects, now leading the way internationally.

1 Bath, Prior Park, 1755
Architect: John Wood Snr
This fine property and bridge were developed by the architect. The landscape architecture was done by Capability Brown.

2

2 Norwich, Elm Hill
A charming, well preserved medieval cobble stoned street.

3 Norwich, Cathedral, 11th-14th Century
One of the finest of early English Gothic.

4

5

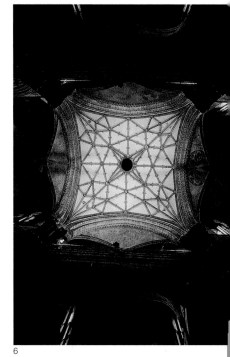

6

Dorset, Shaftsbury, Gold Hill
ith its thatched roofs, it is a favourite
n location.

6 Salisbury, Cathedral, 1220-56
onsidered the purest of English Gothic
chitecture it is cohesive in style, as it
as built in a short time.

Cambridge, Kings College Chapel,
512-15
he perpendicular Gothic fan vaulting was
esigned by John Wastell.

Gloucester, Cathedral Cloister,
360-nearly 1400
arly experimental fan vaulting.

7

8

9

10

9 Ely, Cathedral Octagon, 14th Century
The central tower collapsed and was replaced by the timber framed lantern.

10 Ely, Cathedral Lady Chapel, 15th Century
Vaulting.

11 London, Westminster Abbey, 1245

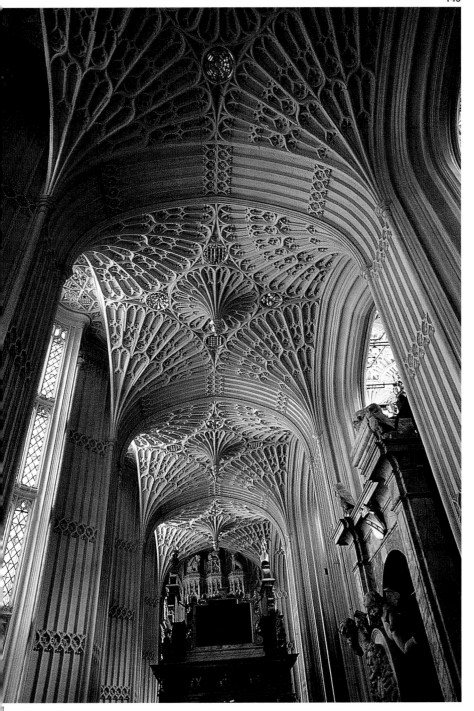

12

13

14

12, 13 East Anglia, Blickling Hall, 16th Century

A Jacobean country house, the one time home of Anne Boleyn, mother of Elizabeth I.

14 Scotland, Drumlanrig Castle, 1679-1691

Distinguished by Baroque horseshoe-shaped entrance stairs and multiple towers.

15 London, Chiswick House, 1725

Architect: Lord Burlington

Country house with perfect ancient Roman and Palladian elements. The focal space is an octagonal domed salon.

16 London, Greenwich, The Grand Hall 1700

Architect: Christopher Wren

5

17 London, Greenwich, The Royal Naval College by Christopher Wren with the Queens House beyond by Inigo Jones, 1620.

18 Oxford, Christ Church Cathedral, 1160

19 Oxford, Radcliffe Camera, 1750
Architect: James Gibbs

20 Oxford, Christ Church Tom Tower, 1681
Architect: Christopher Wren

21 Oxford, Queen's College

22, 23 Bath, The Royal Crescent, 1767
Architect: John Wood the younger
This grandiose town planning assembly of geometric building forms gives an unprecedented cohesive character to the whole town. The housing was built by the Woods, as commercial development.

6

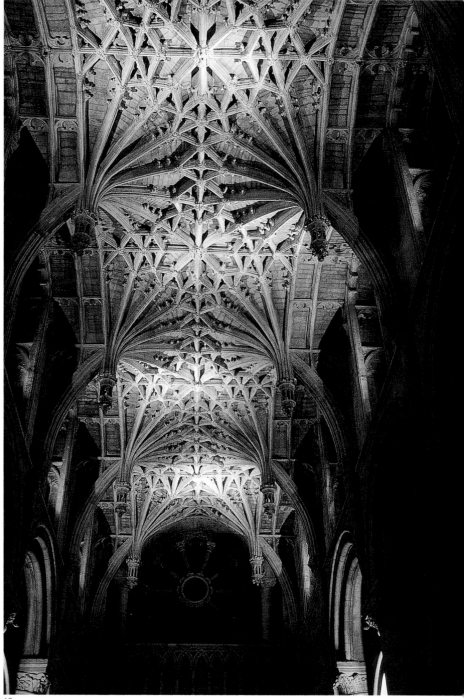

22

23

29

24 London, Carlton House Terrace, The Mall, 1827-33
Architect: John Nash
These formal Classic Buildings form the boulevard leading to Buckingham Palace.

25 London, Regents Park Crescent, 1812
Architect: John Nash
Two colonnaded arc forms face Regents Park, becoming one of the grandest Terrace development of joined houses.

26 London, Pelham Crescent, 1840
Architect: George Basevi

27 London, Royal Opera Arcade, 1818
Architect: John Nash
Strong co-ordinated architectural forms and cohesive timber shop fronts are beautifully maintained.

28 London, Burlington Arcade, 1820
Architect: Samuel Ware
Small finely detailed shops with a glass roof have remained popular for nearly 200 years.

30

29, 30 Ironbridge, 1779
Engineer: Abraham Darby
The world's first iron bridge, which
revolutionised building methods.

31 Glasgow
Unified 19th Century, masonry row
housing and bay windowed glass fronts.

**32 The Glasgow School of Arts,
1897-1909**
Architect: Charles Rennie Mackintosh
The library demonstrates the new spatial
design by the architect, who influenced
pioneering Viennese architecture at the
time.

33

34

33, 35 Brighton, The Royal Pavilion, 1820
Architect: John Nash
This orientally decorated building and its structure, seen in the kitchen, is characteristic of the Prince Regent's exotic taste.

34 Brighton, The Palace Pier, 1899
The focal point of this seaside resort.

36 Brighton
Typical Georgian residence influential to colonial architecture in the 19th Century.

37

38

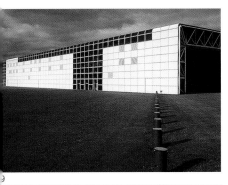

9

37, 39, 40 Norwich, Sainsbury Centre, 1978
Architect: Norman Foster
A technologically advanced structure with co-ordinated solid and glazed components.

38, 41 London, Canary Wharf Station, 1995
Architect: Norman Foster
A monumentally scaled underground station of structurally expressive concrete.

42 Stansted Airport, 1989
Architect: Norman Foster
A rare refined example of airport architecture, free of normal visual confusion and clutter, with all services and signage co-ordinated within the inverted pyramidal shaped sky-lit steel supports.

43 London, British Museum, 2000
Architect: Norman Foster
The courtyard's flat glazed dome inventively uses glass as a structural compressive element.

1

2

45

44, 45 London, Lloyd's Insurance Headquarters, 1982
Architect: Richard Rogers
An important building of advanced technology with expressed structure and mechanical services.

Spain

Spain has had an extraordinary history, var ied with cultural extremes of opposites. T Romans named the land Iberia or Hispan and built roads, bridges and huge engi- neering works such as the stone aquedud in Segovia, which still serves its purpose after 2000 years. Invasions by the Moors from North Africa brought another kind of architecture, which thrived for centuries and stood side by side with fine late Goth structures such as in Seville and Córdoba. The pleasure pavilions in Granada's Alhambra became the most celebrated pieces of architecture in Spain During the cruel, autocratic reign of Philip in the 16th Century, vast Monasteries wer built of solid granite – such as "El Escorial" by virtual slave labour; many died on the building site.

The cities of Spain are graced with wonde ful, huge public plazas – ringed with four sides of co-ordinated buildings. They wer built in the 17th and 18th Centuries and remain the popular focus of their towns. The most extraordinary Catalan architect, nearer our time, was Antoni Gaudí. He designed the church La Sagrada Família i 1883, which is still in construction long af his death. His intuitive structures are emb lished within curvilinear forms, which char acterise all his work.

During the Civil War and in the fascist Franco period, many architects and artist (such as Picasso) chose to live outside Spain. There are few modern buildings of distinction of that period.

1 Barcelona, Casa Milà, 1906-10
Architect: Antoni Gaudí
Detail of Façade

3

2 Barcelona
The Gothic quarter of Barcelona dates back to Roman times, although built in the 13th-15th Centuries.

3 Barcelona
The 15th Century Gothic Cathedral is originally of French design, reconstructed in the 19th Century.

4, 6 Barcelona, La Sagrada Família, 1883 - still in construction
Architect: Antoni Gaudí
This building is the landmark of Barcelona. Long after Gaudí's death the interior structure is finally being completed following the original design but executed in part using pre-cast concrete instead of stone.

5 Barcelona, La Sagrada Família, 1883 - still in construction
Architect: Antoni Gaudí
In spite of its fanciful appearance, it contains rational structural expressions in its column form, predating the work of Piere Luigi Nervi.

7 Barcelona, Casa Milà, 1906-10
Architect: Antoni Gaudí
The unique undulating façade and rooftop sculptural chimneys, this apartment building's character is extended to every detail of the interior.

4

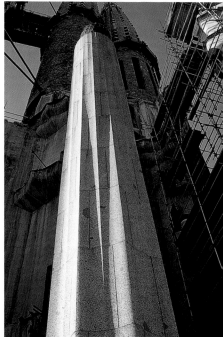

5

Barcelona, Casa Batlló, 1904
rchitect: Antoni Gaudí
he curvilinear stone façade recalls
rganic forms.

Barcelona, Güell Pavilion, 1885
rchitect: Antoni Gaudí
on fence.

0, 11 Barcelona, Casa Milà, 1906-10
rchitect: Antoni Gaudí
he main entrance doors handmade of
eaten wrought iron.

2 Barcelona, Casa Milà, 1906-10
rchitect: Antoni Gaudí
he rooftops sculptural chimneys.

3 Montefrío

4 Toledo

5 Setenil

6 Olvera
outhern Spain's characteristic white hill
owns gain visual consistency using white
ainted walls and terracotta roofs for all
uildings old and new.

7 Castille
olated fortified medieval castle in
e Castille area.

9

10

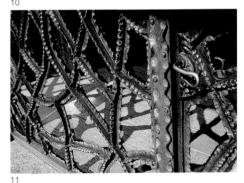

11

12

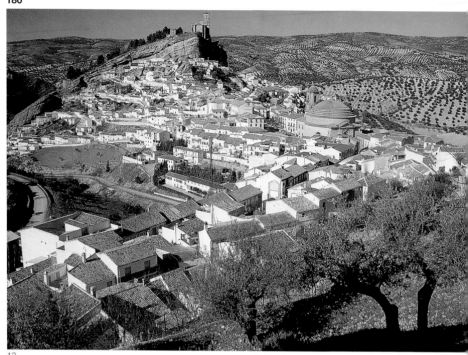

13

14

19

18-21 El Escorial Monastery, 1563
Architect: Juan de Herrera
The sober clean-cut lines of this majestic Monument belie its age. Built entirely of grey granite it achieves the grandeur of a palace and the austerity of a monastery.

20

21

22-24 Segovia, Cathedral, 16th Century
Architect: Juan Gil de Hontañón
A fine late Gothic work.

25 Segovia, Roman Aqueduct
This daring 28 m high structure (1st Century AD) still serves its purpose as an aqueduct.

26, 27 Ronda
This Roman town is built on a platform at the edge of a ravine. It contains the oldest bullring in Spain.

22

23

24

25

26

27

8, 29 Córdoba
or centuries the centre of Muslim Spain.
he huge arched mosque structure, 875-
87 AD, had a Christian Cathedral inserted
ı its centre in the 16th Century.

0 Córdoba
he 13th Century interlocking cross vaults
ге reminiscent of Guarino Guarini's work in
7th Century Turin.

31

31 Granada, Cathedral façade, 17th Century
Architect: Alonso Cano
Seen during a historic celebration.

32-35 Granada, The Alhambra, 1350
An elaborate and richly decorated Muslim fortress palace with formal pavilions; the lion court and the arcaded Myrtles court with a central reflecting pool.

32

36

37

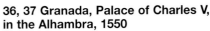

36, 37 Granada, Palace of Charles V, in the Alhambra, 1550
Architect: Pedro & Luis Machuca
A square Renaissance building, with an internal arcaded circular court.

38 Burgos, Town Gate
14th Century

39, 40 Madrid, Plaza Mayor, 1620
Architect: Juan Gomez de Mora
This public square surrounded by fine buildings forms the focus of Habsburg Madrid, and it is used for celebrations.

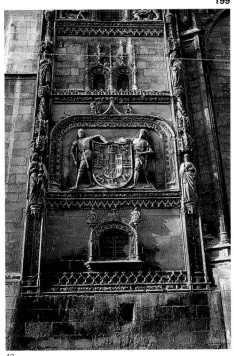

42

41 Burgos, Cathedral, 1490
Architect: Simon de Colonia
The octagonal Chapel Contestable.

42 Burgos, Cathedral
Sculptured Coroneria doorway.

43 Salamanca, Plaza Mayor, 1730
Architect: Churriguera Bros
One of the finest squares in Spain much
frequented by University students.

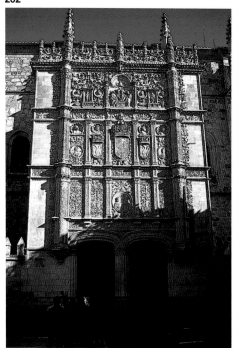

44

45

46

47

48

49

44 Salamanca, University, 1520
Sculpted entrance façade.

**45-47 Salamanca, New Cathedral,
started 1513**
Architect: Juan Gil de Hontanon
The decorative fan vaulting extends
into the transept.

48, 49 Ávila
This picturesque, intact, fortified
11th Century town has accessible
continuous ramparts.

50-53 Barcelona, German Pavilion, 1929
Architect: Ludwig Mies van der Rohe

This ultimate icon of modern architecture was erected for the International exhibition in 1929, demolished after a mere three months and faithfully reconstructed permanently as a museum in 1986.

The concentration of support in regularly placed steel columns allowed the free disposition, independently, of screen-like walls that create a continuum of flowing space between them.

This spatial openness is dramatised by the use of the most sumptuous materials, polished marble, onyx, travertine and polished chrome. Two reflecting pools complete this dramatic demonstration of the new language in architecture, amplified by the architect's specially designed chairs, which have become famous internationally. There are no exhibits in the building, which in itself serves that purpose. The black carpet, yellow leather upholstery on the chairs and a red curtain, the colours of the German flag, confirm this.

50

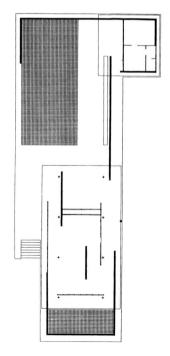

51

54

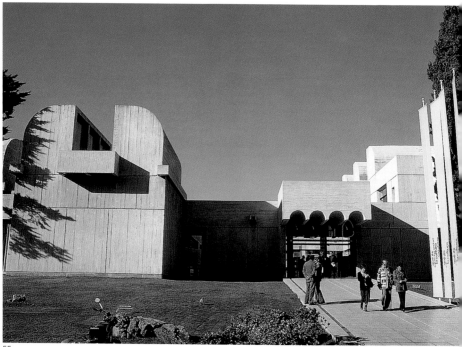

55

54, 56, 57 Bilbao, Underground Station, 1991
Architect: Norman Foster
Approached through glass arched entries from street level, the upper station concourse is suspended from the wide precast concrete vaulted station roof.

55 Barcelona, Miró Foundation, 1976
Architect: José Luis Sert
The museum is dedicated to Sert's friend and countryman, the Spanish artist Miró. The various pavilions showing different phases of Miró's work are top lit from segmental concrete vaults, which throw diffused daylight onto the artworks and create a rich spaciousness within.

58 Bilbao, Footbridge, 1997
Engineer: Santiago Calatrava
This extraordinary structure has the translucent glass walkway (dramatically lit from within at night) suspended from a one-sided tilting arch support.

60

59-61 Bilbao, Guggenheim Museum, 1997

Architect: Frank Gehry

This amazing unprecedented sculptural building is made possible in our computer era which not only enables architects to draw such designs accurately, but by the computer instructing machines to produce all elements for assembly. There are virtually no straight or perpendicular lines in the building. The exterior is sheathed with panels of Titanium.

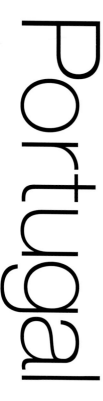

Portugal

Even though Portugal has some of the richest examples of Gothic and Baroque Building Art, their importance and historic value have largely gone unnoticed. It seem that historians did not visit Portugal and have always concentrated on other centres of European architectural culture.

The country's rich background dates from the golden age of Portuguese discoveries when its navigators set sail to explore the New World. This gained its huge wealth from trade in spices from the East and gold and sugar from plantations in colonial Brazil. The wealth made possible the many distinctive, well preserved monuments.

Due to the country's warm and sunny climate, central European architectural styles through the ages were transformed into more open and different configurations.

A traditional craft, the production of fine blue "Azulejos" wall tiles used to cover large exterior wall areas, gives a unique characte to Portuguese historic buildings.

The Baroque buildings of the 17th and 18t Centuries, in comparison to those of centr Europe, create an extraordinary flamboyan sculptural imagery, which find their parallel in the historic towns of Brazil.

Tomar, Azulejos Wall

Batalha, Cloister, 1500

4

3, 4 Belém, Monastery of Jeronimos, 1495-1521
Architect: Diogo de Boytac
An example of Manueline Architecture with distinctive rib vaulting and cloisters.

5-8 Tomar, Church of Nossa Senhora, 12th Century
With an intricately carved façade, ribbed vaulting, curved stone stairs and Azulejo tiled cloistered courtyards.

7

9 Coimbra, 18th Century
A fine 17th Century Manueline chapel by
Marcos Pires decorated with Azulejos.

10,12 Batalha, Santa Maria da Vitória
The late 14th Century monastery and
church built by an Irishman in flamboyant
Gothic style for the English Queen Philippa
of Lancaster. The Royal Cloister is
surrounded by carved marble arcades.

**11 Coimbra, Monastery of the Holy
Cross, 16th Century**
With a freestanding Renaissance portico.

9

10

11

12

13

14

3 Óbidos Castle
The medieval building was transformed into
a palace in the 16th Century, built against
the old town wall.

4 Porto
A huge Azulejos tiled exterior church wall.

5 Buçaco Forest
Fed by a natural spring, the "Cold
Fountain", flanked by staircases on both
sides, cascades down in the magnificent
forest.

6 Porto, Dom Luis I Bridge, 1886
Engineer: Theophile Seyrig
This iron engineering feat has two
superimposed roads, connecting both
upper and lower levels of the town on
either side of the river.

7 Braga, Bom Jesus do Monte
Architect: Carlos Amarante
The twin towered 18th Century pilgrimage
church stands atop a granite and plaster
Baroque staircase, adorned with fountains
and terracotta statues. The form of this
long double stair built into the natural
hillside is one of the richest examples of
Baroque art.

15

16

Netherlands

To most visitors, the cities of the Netherlands, especially Amsterdam, conjure up the image of tree lined canals with charming narrow fronted row houses on both sides; hence the name "The Venice of the North" Although this ubiquitous historic character is typical, the emergence of the Architectural "Amsterdam School" at the beginning of the 20th Century is prevalent in more recent buildings. It is a solid style of socially "comfortable" buildings with a few individual architects raising it to architectural importance. The best known of these is Hendrik Berlage, the architect of the Amsterdam Stock Exchange, which is a powerful large building of brick, inside and out, of visible structural expression and no applied decoration. The few carved embellishments are set into the fabric of the building to form an integral part of it.

In the 1920s and 30s, the "De Stijl" movement, both in painting and architecture, produced some buildings of world importance, which influenced architecture in the rest of the western world, even to this day. Aside from Dutch artists such as Piet Mondrian and Theo van Doesburg, a revolutionary small house and its furniture designed by Gerrit Rietveld in Utrecht, and the work of Jacobus Johannes Pieter Oud have influenced modern building throughout the country.

Developing in parallel with the new art and architecture at the Bauhaus in Germany, some large pioneering buildings stand out as landmark structures which are now as valid visually and physically as they were in the 1920s such as the famous van Nelle factory in Rotterdam by Brinkman and van der Vlugt, or the Bergpolder, Gallery-Access Apartments by Willem van Tijen.

1 Rotterdam, van Nelle Factory, 1924
Architects: Brinkman & van der Vlugt
One of the earliest total glass curtain wall
buildings in Europe expressly designed for
the comfort and safety of employees.

2

2 Amsterdam, Open Air School, 1930
Architect: Johannes Duiker
An early reinforced concrete glazed structure with cantilevered corners. The building is as new, still used for its original purpose.

3 Amsterdam
Narrow fronted buildings along canals with characteristically Dutch gables, large windows and lifting beams projecting from the roof to raise furniture.

4 Amsterdam
Typical tree lined canal with joined buildings on both sides.

5 Amsterdam, Stock Exchange, 1903
Architect: Hendrik Petrus Berlage
An early minimalist structurally expressive brick building.

7

6, 7 Utrecht, Schröder House, 1924
Architect: Gerrit Rietveld
The most famous of "De Stijl" buildings with
a flexible subdividable open interior is a
publicly accessible museum.
Opposing vertical and horizontal slab-like
walls and continuous glass areas create
compositions with their "tensional" window
sub-divisions, which recall the work of
Dutch artists at the time.

Belgium

This small multilingual country can boast a fine, exceptionally tall, Gothic Cathedral in Antwerp and the 17th Century Guild Houses ringing Brussels' Grand Place, as its historic heritage. The Guild Houses have richly decorated gabled facades, some adorned with gold leaf, between their large windows. The facades are all different and yet form a unified totality in this focal point of Brussels. The unique architectural development, however, emerged at the turn of the 19th and early 20th Centuries in the work of Victor Horta, exemplified in his own house, which is now a public museum. His work is a rare combination of flamboyant "Art Nouveau" linear decoration (such as on stair railings and lamp posts), with deliberately exposed iron structural elements, columns and girders. These proudly show the pattern of their riveted connections, all intertwined with the swirling curvilinear patterns of Horta's special kind of strap iron ornamentation. The strength of this work is based on the contrast of plain wall surfaces of stone, tiles or brick, with the unrolled curls and rosettes of his linear metal embellishments.

Beyond the materials and the decorative combinations they are given, it is the new Space Horta creates in his buildings that particularly herald the future.

In his own house the central stair gives access to open split-level arrangements of rooms leading from it. This allows for continuous spaciousness to emerge, even in the limited size of his buildings. Such fusing of levels and spaces became the hallmark of modern architecture more than two decades later.

1 Brussels, Solvay House, 1896
Architect: Victor Horta
The polished stone stair and walls are combined with characteristic flat iron ornate railing. They are in contrast to the exposed riveted steel columns and beams.

2

3

4

2-4 Brussels, Horta House, 1898
Architect: Victor Horta
The central curved stair with flat iron decoration, gives access to split-level floors, creating a continuity of spatial effects. Walls are of bare glazed brick and tiles reaching the top floor with a curved glass skylight.

5

5 Brussels, 17th Century
Guild Houses ringing the Grand Place with
gold leaf decoration between large windows.

6 Antwerp
Gothic Cathedral with its central tall tower.

7 Antwerp
The town square with touching
gabled facades.

Denmark

Denmark's architecture is related to that of other Scandinavian countries. The richly decorated gables of historic structures are punctuated by high spires, the most famous being Copenhagen's 16th Century stock exchange's spiral tower.

The country has consistently produced excellent modern buildings, particularly by the architect Arne Jacobson, whose furniture and the design of objects of use are known worldwide.

The most brilliant of Danish architects, however, is Jørn Utzon, who won the international competition for the Sydney Opera House, which has become the very icon of Australia. After leaving that project, due to controversy prior to its completion, he proceeded to create some wonderful buildings and furniture elsewhere. One of the finest is the Bagsvaerd Church and the exemplary Fredensborg group housing near Copenhagen. It showed the practical and aesthetic advantages of such housing rather than routine suburbia.

1 Copenhagen, Nyhavn
The picturesque canal dating from the 17th Century, which has become a popular pedestrian promenade and boat anchorage.

2 Copenhagen
The charming central pedestrian district.

3

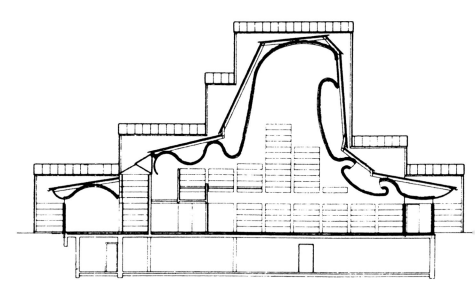

4

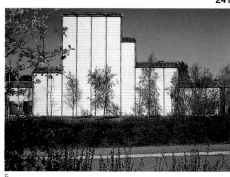

5

6

3-6 Copenhagen, Bagsvaerd Church, 1976
Architect: Jørn Utzon
One of the finest works of Utzon after leaving the Sydney Opera House project. The wave-like form of the interior is surrounded by a stepped rectilinear structure, and enclosed courts that create a unique dichotomy of spaces.

Finland

Formerly part of Sweden, Finland became an autonomous part of Russia and Helsinki its capital. The new Neo-Classical centre was built largely by the German architect Carl Engel, the focal point of which is the hilltop Lutheran Cathedral of 1830. Its sparkling white and gilded exterior still dominate the city.

The design competition for the Central Railway Terminal was won in 1904 by Eliel Saarinen (the father of Eero Saarinen who later produced some fine architecture in the USA). The building, completed in 1914, shows Art Nouveau stylistic influences, which dominated whole districts of Helsinki. As in many of his other buildings, the use of solid granite exteriors has made it remain in pristine condition for nearly a century. Geographically isolated from the rest of Europe, Finland was late to be industrialised. It maintained its handicraft tradition until the 1920s, which gave rise to the creation of the finest modern design products in the world today; textiles, glassware, crockery, cutlery, furniture, etc.

The leading figure in Finnish architecture and furniture design was Alvar Aalto who influenced a whole generation of modern architects world wide, evidenced by the high standard of design and town planning in the country.

Tapiola
ypical groups of apartments set in un-
ouched pine tree forests and granite out-
rops.

Helsinki, Lutheran Cathedral, 1830-52
rchitect: Carl Engel
he glistening white classic building stands
n a commanding hilltop.

4

3 Helsinki, Central Railway Terminal, 1910
Architect: Eliel Saarinen
The solid granite building with Art Nouveau sculptures and decoration.

4 Helsinki, National Museum, 1902-10
Architect: Eliel Saarinen
Has a finely carved granite façade, especially a bear, which is a Finnish symbol.

5

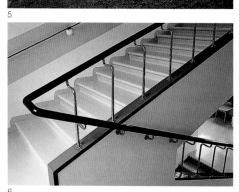

6

5, 6 Paimio, Sanatorium, 1929-33
Architect: Alvar Aalto
Standing in a remote forest of tall pine trees, this present day fully functioning pristine white building complex, belies its age inside and out. The interiors are cheerfully bright and colourful.

7 Helsinki Olympic Stadium Tower, 194(
Architects: Yrjö Lindegren & Toivo Jäntti
The 72 m high elegantly slim concrete outlook tower was completed for the 1940 Olympic Games, which due to the war were not held there until 1952.

8

8 Tapiola Centre

Community buildings, a church, the Espoo cultural centre (Architect Arto Sipinen, 1989) a public pool, etc, are built around a lake, which had been an unused brick pit. In my view, the environment created in the totally planned new town of Tapiola achieves the highest physical standard for civilised life, anywhere in today's world.

9, 10 Tapiola, 1950s
Planner/Architect: Arne Ervi
This Garden City, set in natural surroundings, is an extension area 10 km from Helsinki. It contains a variety of courtyard houses, spaciously placed waterfront townhouses and apartment blocks.

Austria

As I was born in Vienna and lived there until the age of 15, I feel a particular affinity with the City, which I grew to love as much as the spectacular mountain scenery in the countryside of Austria.

Vienna has a long and dramatic history. It started as the town Vindobona in Roman times and centuries later developed into the capital of a large empire that covered much of Europe, from the Veneto to the border with Russia until its dismemberment into a small country after World War I.

What is left to us of Vienna, the capital of a once wealthy empire, is a city serving a small country with the heritage of extravagant palaces and churches.

Massive Gothic Cathedrals and Monasteries were built in the 12th and 13th Century with beautifully rib-vaulted naves and equal height aisles, and also the distinctively picturesque onion-domed towers of village churches throughout the mountainous provinces.

A great building boom started in the period of peace following the defeat of the Turkish armies in 1683 that had laid siege to Vienna.

Surrounding the "Hofburg", the seat of the Hapsburg Rulers, palaces were built by the Nobles throughout the medieval city centre which was surrounded by high fortification walls. In this, during the 18th Century high Baroque period, elaborate churches and ambitious establishments of the aristocracy came into being. The celebrated architects of the time, such as Fischer von Erlach and Lucas von Hildebrandt are responsible for the Spanish Riding School, the National Library, the Schönbrum summer palace, etc.

In mid 19th Century the wall surrounding the city was razed and a wide boulevard, the "Ringstraße" took its place, lined with sumptuous civic buildings; the Parliament, the famous Opera House, museums (housing the Habsburg art collection), the City Hall, theatres, the University, etc.

At the turn of the 20th Century, the ferment of feverish artistic activity created a reaction against conservative Classicism in the arts, particularly in architecture, symbolised by the Sezession movement and its exhibition uilding's famous inscription "To each era s art and to art its freedom". With this redo, the foundations of modern architecture were laid by such luminaries as Otto Wagner, Adolf Loos and Josef Hoffmann. Following the First World War, to alleviate the dreadful housing conditions, the newly proclaimed republic dedicated itself to the building of public housing for all. More than half of Vienna's population now lives in such housing in exemplary planned areas that to date have no equal in the rest of the civilised world.

1

1 Krems
The town portal with Medieval and Baroque decorative towers.

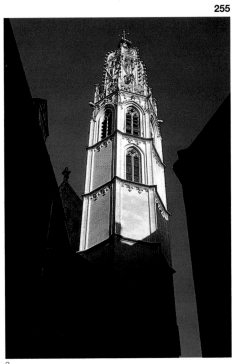

3

2, 3 Maria am Gestade, 15th Century
Structurally expressive ribbed vaulting and
Gothic decorated tower.

4

5

4 Wachau Church
Equally high Gothic vaulting over nave and aisles.

5 Salzburg
Gothic vaulting.

6 Dürnstein
The 15th Century church was rebuilt in the Baroque period, standing on the edge of the Donau, below the high up castle where Richard Lionheart was kept prisoner in the 12th Century.

7 Stein
Façade with applied Baroque ornament.

10

8, 9 Vienna, Jesuit Church, 1626-31
The richly gilded interior is crowned
by a Trompe-l'œil dome fresco by
Andrea Pozzo.

10 Vienna, St Peter's Church, 1702-30
Architect: Lucas von Hildebrandt
The exterior with its inward tilted towers
and concave front façade make the
building fit comfortably into the restrictive
site.

2

1 Vienna, St Stephan's Cathedral

The 14th Century Cathedral stands in an extensive pedestrian precinct. The glazed modern Haas House façade opposite the Cathedral would not be permitted in most cities. It adds to the rich mixture of surrounding important buildings dating from different centuries.

2 Vienna, Spanish Riding School, 18th Century

Architect: Fischer von Erlach

The white colonnaded wide span long hall is home to the unique performances of Lippizaner horses trained to do difficult jumps, steps and dances, all in unison with musical accompaniment.

13

13, 14 Vienna, Piaristen Church, 1700
Architect: Lucas von Hildebrandt
The brilliant Baroque spatial interior has
indirect natural light reaching the central
nave from hidden overhead sources.

15 Vienna, Karlskirche, 1715
Architect: Fischer von Erlach
This amazing Baroque church has a
classic temple portico flanked by two
freestanding minaret-like pylons leading
to a high oval domed interior.

16

17

16, 17 Vienna, Liechtenstein Palais, 1700
Architect: Domenico Martinelli
A grand staircase rises to the central hall decorated with a perspective ceiling fresco by Andrea Pozzo.

18 Vienna, Armoury, Am Hof, 1731-32
Architect: Anton Ospel
Originally built as a civil armoury, since 1870 it is used as Vienna's ornate Fire Brigade Headquarters.

19 Melk, Benedictine Monastery, early 18th Century
Architect: Jacob Prandtauer
Dramatically sited on a high rocky ledge above the Danube, the monumental church interior is sumptuously gilded, as is the adjacent library.

20, 21 Vienna, Belvedere Palace, 1721
Architect: Lucas von Hildebrandt
Built for Prince Eugene of Savoy in gratitude after his defeat of the Turks who surrounded the city in 1683. The palace has a commanding view of Vienna over its formal gardens and fountains, which have not changed since Bellotto (called Canaletto) painted the scene in the 18th Century.

22

23

22, 23 Vienna, Schönbrunn Summer Palace, 1680-1740
Architects: Fischer von Erlach and Nikolaus Parcassi
The Empress Maria Theresa was determined to outdo Louis 14th's Palace at Versailles. Even though Schönbrunn is smaller, it has more charm and human scale. The interiors are sumptuously appointed and the axial formal gardens focus on the Gloriette (architect von Hohenberg) built on high ground.

24, 25 Vienna, Schönbrunn Palm House, 1880-1882
Architect: Franz von Segenschmid

4

5

26

27

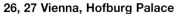

26, 27 Vienna, Hofburg Palace
The historic residence of the Emperor was built in many stages from the 15th to the early 20th Century in various wings around formal courts.

28, 29 Vienna, Kinsky Palace, 1713-16
Architect: Lucas von Hildebrandt
The city residence of a Noble has a grand staircase crowned with a fresco by Chiarini.

30

30 Vienna, Pestsäule, 1693
Architect: Fischer von Erlach
Erected on the Graben Plaza to give thanks
at the end of the plague, which had
decimated the population.

31 St. Florian Abbey Library, 1690
Architect: Jacob Prandtauer

32 Hallstadt
Romantically picturesque town on
the edge of a lake at the foothills of the
Dachstein Mountain.

33 Vienna, Kunsthistorisches Museum, 1875

Architects: Carl von Hasenauer and Gottfried Semper

The grandiose classic building houses the Habsburg's important and extensive art collection.

34 Vienna, Steinhof Church, 1905-07

Architect: Otto Wagner

Even though the silhouette of the domed church appears classical, the embellishments and especially the interior speak a totally new visual language; white marble, gilding and Secessionist forms.

33

34

35 Vienna, Ringstraße

After the demolition of the medieval fortification walls in 1858, the Parliament (1874, architect Theophil Hansen) and other public buildings and parks were built along the resulting wide tree-lined Boulevard.

36 Vienna, Stadtpark

Gilded monument to Johann Strauss.

37

37 Vienna, Postsparkasse, 1906
Architect: Otto Wagner
This most inventive and progressive
building for its time has a glass roofed
banking hall and specially designed air
heating columns, light fixtures and
furniture.
The thick granite exterior facing is secured
with exposed metal bolts.

38 Vienna, Loos Haus, 1910
Architect: Adolf Loos
The first, totally undecorated façade
opposite the Hofburg, the Imperial Palace
offended the Emperor. The architect
had to add window flower boxes.

38

9

39 Vienna, Karl-Marx-Hof, 1926
Architect: Karl Ehn
One of the first of many public housing
projects built by the City following the
establishment of the Republic after World
War I. 60% of the Viennese now live in
such housing.

40

41

42

43

44

45

40, 41 Vienna, Wienzeile Apartments, 1898
Architect: Otto Wagner
The façade is decorated with gilded plaster. The interior iron elevator and stair railings break with tradition.

42 Vienna, Hof Pavilion, 1898
Architect: Otto Wagner
The private underground train station built near the Schönbrunn Palace for the Emperor, with Art Nouveau inspired decoration.

43 Vienna, Karlsplatz Underground Station, 1898
Architect: Otto Wagner
The gilded iron framed structure holds walls of white marble panels, said to be the first non-weight bearing "curtain wall".

44 Vienna, Flood Control Building, 1906
Architect: Otto Wagner

45, 46 Vienna, Sezession Exposition Pavilion, 1898
Architect: Joseph Maria Olbrich
With the famous inscription "To each era its art and to art its freedom".

47

48

49

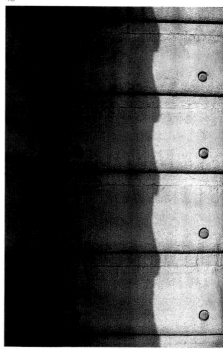

50

51

47-50 Vienna, Postsparkasse, 1906
Architect: Otto Wagner
Specially designed air heating columns, light fixtures and furniture. The thick granite exterior facing is secured with exposed metal bolts.

51 Vienna, Candle Shop, 1964-66
Architect: Hans Hollein
The façade is entirely of jointlessly fused aluminium sheets.

52 Vienna, Holocaust Memorial, 2000
Artist: Rachel Whiteread
The solid stone exterior is all carved without openings. The doors are solid, and the walls are in the shape of inverted books – all is hidden, inaccessible and inexplicable forever.

Switzerland

It is hard for this small country to compete with the historic architecture of its large neighbours, France, Germany and Italy. Without their war damage, however, the medieval charm of Swiss towns and the breathtaking mountainous scenery are hard to beat. There are some exceptions such as the extraordinary Einsiedeln Benedictine Abbey with its Baroque interior planned around a pilgrimage area in its centre. Modern architecture developed a strong foothold in the 1930s with the application of high quality technology and characteristically solid construction evident, particularly in their new schools and public buildings. The wealth of the country resulted in patrons commissioning some of the best progressive architects to design their houses and buildings, such as Le Corbusier and Marcel Breuer.

Outstanding amongst the local creative talents is the pioneering structural engineer Robert Maillart whose bridges span the deep chasms in the Swiss Alps and the artist and architect Max Bill.

Zurich

2

3

2-5 Einsiedeln, Benedictine Abbey, 1704-47

Architect: Kaspar Moosbrugger
Dominating the large town square, the church's unusual plan places the pilgrimage area in the centre of a large oval entrance space. This results in a dramatically radiating arched support structure. To increase the apparent depth of the nave is an iron screen, with lines imitating perspective effects.

6 Geneva, Vessy Bridge, 1936
Engineer: Robert Maillart
A seminal example by a pioneer of a concrete structure that is expressive of rational static forces and simultaneously achieves fine visual results.

7 Zürich, Doldertal Apartments, 1935
Architect: Marcel Breuer
The two identical residential buildings face a steep wooded river valley. They are celebrated icons of early modern architecture.

6

7

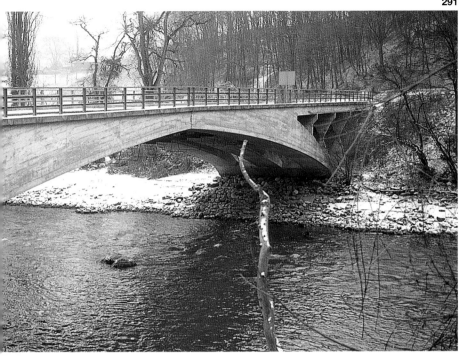

8

9

8, 9 Moscia, Koerfer House, 1963
Architect: Marcel Breuer
Built on a rugged hillside commanding a
sweeping view of Lago Maggiore, the
concrete structure is exposed both inside
and out. It stands on granite rubble walls,
which fit the house into the terrain.

10 Zürich, La Maison de l'Homme, 1967
Architect: Le Corbusier
The exhibition pavilion is the result of the
private initiative of Heidi Weber and was
built in a public park close to Zürich Lake.
One of the few steel structures by Le
Corbusier, its form is defined by two
opposing umbrella-like roof forms. The
brightly coloured exterior panels contrast
with the off-form concrete access ramp.

Czech Republic

This small country has a varied history. Before World War I, it was a part of the Habsburg Empire, then a joined part with its neighbour Slovakia and now on its own. It is known not only for its beautiful small towns dating from the middle ages, but also for its technologically advanced industries and universities.

The World War II German army's advance to the east caused little damage to the World Heritage old towns such as Telc, Cesky Budevice, Cesky Krumlov, etc. Since the end of the Iron Curtain, Prague has become the treasure house of architectural heritage from Gothic, Baroque and the modern era.

St Vitus Cathedral from the 14th Century, the Hradcany Castle's rib-vaulted King's Hall and the charming alchemists' tiny houses next to the palace, are all unique. Aside from the classical Baroque churches built in the 18th Century, the little known architect Jan Santini produced some amazing buildings such as the church in Zdar. One of the first large modern public buildings, the Pensions Institute of 1924 (architects Havlicek and Honzik) is evidence of the country being the first to adopt modern architecture wholeheartedly.

Recognised throughout the civilised world as the very icon of modern architecture is the Tugendhat House, 1929, by Mies van der Rohe, built in Brno. It is not only an aesthetic triumph, but the methods and materials used would strain the resources of today, 75 years later.

Prague
Old Town Square with the 15th Century
Tyn Church.

2

2 Prague, Cernin Palace

3 Prague, Castle entrance

4 Prague
Three façades in Old Town Square, dating from 14th to 18th Century.

5

5, 7 Prague, St Nicholas Church, 1700
Architect: Christoph Dientzenhofer
A superbly flamboyant example of Baroque architecture inside and out.

6, 8 Prague, St Vitus Cathedral, 14th Century
Architects: Peter Parler and Matthias of Arras
The structure spanning the high nave and crossing consists of exceptionally narrow columns and high clerestory, rising to interlocking ribbed vaults.

9, 10 Prague Castle, Vladislav Hall
15th-16th Century
Architect: Benedikt Rejt
The exposed curved vaulting ribs are largely decorative and of doubtful structural value.

11, 12 Prague, Strahov Abbey and
Philosophical Hall, 18th Century
Ceiling fresco by A. F. Maulbertsch.

9

10

13 Cesky Krumlov, St Vitus Church, 1439

14 Brno Cathedral, 15th Century
Architect: Anthony Pilgram

15 Kutna Hora, St Barbara Cathedral, 1380
Architect: Matyas Rejsek
The delicately interwoven vault ribbing.

16 Telc
The main square in this World Heritage listed town is ringed by continuous arcaded buildings. Although they have different facades, the result is a harmonious totality.

17

18

9

17 Telc

18 Slavonice
16th Century "diamond" vaulting in a
building entry court.

19 Cesky Budevice
The huge square surrounded by arcaded
buildings and the Town Hall form the
popular focus of this small town.

20, 21 Zdar, St Nepomuk Church, 1722
Architect: Jan Santini
This five-sided domed church (a UNESCO
Cultural Heritage) is based on extraordinary
geometry, which changes from the inside to
the richly sculptural exterior. Surrounding
the churchyard is a typical Santini work with
chapels of alternating concave and convex
plan outlines.

22, 24-26 Brno, Tugendhat House, 1929
Architect: Ludwig Mies van der Rohe
This house built for the Tugendhat family in 1929 is one of Mies van der Rohe's masterpieces. The free-flowing spaces are made possible by the use of technologically advanced construction for its time, such as exposed chromed steel supports and enormous areas of glass, which can be electrically lowered down below the floor. Neglected and vandalised during World War II, it is now a faithfully restored house museum, furnished with the famous tables and chairs Mies designed specially for the house. Onyx and Palisander screen walls create a sumptuously elegant atmosphere, which is an icon in modern architecture.

23 Ludwig Mies van der Rohe, 1886-1969

27 Marienbad Colonnade, 1889
Architects: Miksch and Niedzielski
This popular spa, set in a park, is typical of the late 19th Century. The long ambulatory is of ornate cast iron construction.

22

23

24

Hungary

This small country has a unique background, starting with the Magyar people's migration from central Asia, the language they brought (with its only parallel in Finland) and the 150 year long occupation by the Turks. All these contributed to a vibrant architectural development over the centuries.

After the Turks were driven out in 1686 the country came under Habsburg rule, and was absorbed into the Austro-Hungarian Monarchy.

Budapest, the second capital in the Empire has many parallel characteristics to those of Vienna; an almost identical Opera House and similar palaces of members of the aristocracy.

The outstanding and most ambitious of these who built estates are members of the Esterhazy dynasty. The rivalry between the two countries is given expression in Prince Miklos Esterhazy's famous challenge, vying to outdo each other "Anything the Habsburgs can afford, I can too". After building design during the 19th Century followed the modes of Classicism and Gothic Revival, a number of Hungarian architects were some of the first to practic modern architecture in Europe. The best-known of these are two who became key figures at the German Bauhaus, Marcel Breuer in architecture and furniture design, and Lazlo Maholy-Nagy in art.

1 Fertőd, Esterhazy Palace, 1760
Reminiscent of Vienna's Schönbrunn Palace down to the yellow-ochre exterior colouring.

2 Budapest, Heroes Square, 1886
Architect: Schickendanz
With statues of Hungary's greatest leaders from the founding of the State to the 19th Century.

3 Budapest, Neo Gothic Parliament Building "Orszaghaz", 1885-1902
Architect: Imre Steindl
Built on a dramatic waterfront site facing the Danube.

3

5

4 Budapest, Museum of Applied Arts, 1883-1896
Architect: Ödön Lechner
Curvilinear central interior space, to emphasise the eastern origin of the country.

5 Budapest
Cast iron candelabra on the Café Hungaria building.

Bulgaria

Being on the international route from Eastern and Central Europe to Asia Minor and the Middle East, Bulgaria's architecture shows diverse influences. A strong Roman tradition left a predominance of arched structures, aqueducts, amphitheatres and thermae. Byzantine domed structures recall the long lasting invasions of Ottoman Turks. Culturally, the country has had a strong affinity with Russia. The most distinctive building complexes are the numerous Monasteries throughout the country. Often built in isolated mountainous regions, which were liable to attack, they were built with bland and solid high surrounding walls. Life was turned inward onto large courtyards lined with arched access galleries. The focal point of the establishments is always the Church, freestanding and sculpturally elaborate, resulting in a distinctive island-like totality.

1 Sofia
The city square with the Gold Domed Alexander Nevski Cathedral, 1912, and the central Parliament House.

2 Plovdiv
The Roman Amphitheatre built by Philip II of Macedonia.

3, 5 Plovdiv
Typical of the 19th Century revival school architecture with flamboyantly decorated curvilinear facades.

4 St Kirik Monastery
A fortified medieval monastery with an 11th Century church in the central court.

6 Rila Monastery, 13th-14th Century
This listed world monument of culture is built around a large internal court with an angular sited Byzantine church at its focus. The surrounding arcaded galleries give the only access to the monastery's rooms. For protection, the exterior walls of the complex are blank.

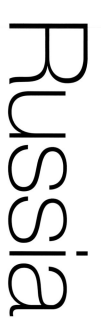

Russia

It was the ambition of Peter the Great to bring Russia closer to Europe that resulted in the founding of St Petersburg in 1703 and being proclaimed the new Russian capital in 1712.

The grandiose palaces standing in huge public spaces and the spiky tower of the admiralty, built along the Neva, are the architectural highlights of the city and attest to a great urban vision. The Italian architect B.F. Rastrelli was responsible for the Hermitage Winter Palace fronting the historic palace square and gilded interiors filled with priceless artworks, the Catherine Palace and the Smolny Cathedral and Convent, all built between 1750-1760.

Rastrelli also built the Peterhof surrounded by innumerable fountains and cascades, the totality rightly called the Russian Versailles. The palace was heavily damaged in World War II but was reconstructed.

Moscow was the first city in the world to invite Le Corbusier to actually build a large government complex in the 1920s, the Centrosoyus. This was indicative of the country's promising avant-garde constructivist movement in the arts of the 1920s, exemplified by the work of Malevich, Kandinsky and Rodchenko.

In the 1930s this came to an end when Stalin stopped progress and decreed reversion to classical building forms. Seven wedding-cake-like skyscrapers were built in the 1950s and remain to this day, as reminders of the absurd results of dictatorship's misguided edicts in art and architecture.

The Kremlin in Moscow contains the city's most impressive buildings. The walled precinct contains a group of 15th Century gilded domed churches, the purest of them being the vaulted Assumption Cathedral. The immense extent of Red Square with the bizarre, St Basil's Cathedral at one end is the very centre of the city. The wealth of the 19th Century is reflected in the Gum Department Store, which forms one full length of the Square. The glass vaulted iron construction is reminiscent of earlier shopping arcades in Milan and Naples.

1 St Petersburg, Hermitage Winter Palace, 1764
Architect: Bartolomeo Francesco Rastrelli
The long building facing the river on one side and the historic square on the other, is a sumptuously appointed structure with internal courtyards.

2 St Petersburg
The historic square with the 47 m high Alexander column, commemorating the 1812 victory over Napoleon.

3 St Petersburg
The Hermitage's river façade.

4

5

4, 5 St Petersburg, Hermitage
The monumental entrance with gilded
decor.

6 St Petersburg
Peter the Great's "The Bronze Horseman"
statue, facing the Neva.

7 St Petersburg
The reconstructed Peterhof Palace with
fountains playing and ballet dancers
performing celebrating an anniversary.

8 St Petersburg
Museums and Palaces facing the Neva.

9 St Petersburg, Catherine Palace
The long façade overlooking the park
setting.

8

9

11

12

10 St Petersburg, Catherine Palace
Details of the reconstructed façade.

11 St Petersburg, Catherine Palace
The Great Hall

12 St Petersburg, Catherine Palace
The reconstructed Amber Room, which
was destroyed during World War II.

**13 Smolny, Cathedral and Convent,
1764**
Architect: Bartolomeo Francesco Rastrelli
The Cathedral is the centrepiece of the
large group of buildings. Rastrelli aimed
to combine Baroque detail with a forest
of onion domes of a traditional Russian
monastery.

14

15

16

17

14 St Petersburg, Catherine Palace
The Grotto pavilion on the lake in the park
surrounding the Palace.

15 St Petersburg, Catherine Palace,
Pavilion in the Palace Park, 1750
Architect: Charles Cameron
The gallery building is only an arcade
to connect the palace with the park.

16, 17 Moscow
Underground Stations, built in the
1930s with elaborate traditional marble
decoration to evoke an atmosphere of
palatial splendour for the masses of users.

19

18 Moscow, Kremlin, Assumption Cathedral, 1470
The beautifully proportioned arched façade is crowned with gold surfaced circular towers.

19 Moscow, Kremlin, Archangel Cathedral

20 Moscow, Red Square
The focal point of the city, with the colourfully decorated domes of St Basil's Cathedral and people lining up to see Lenin's tomb.

21 Moscow, GUM Department Store, 1895
Architect: Alexander Pomerantsev
Along Red Square, is an elaborate complex of iron and glass vaulted shopping galleries.

Turkey

What emerges from the country's thousands of years of colonisation, wars and occupation is one amazing building, built under Emperor Justinian in about 550 AD, Hagia Sophia in Constantinople (now Istanbul).

There had been various attempts at ambitious church construction on its site for 30 years, resulting in successive structural failures. Even though the area is subject to earthquakes, Justinian's daring constructic has survived with some structural addition It remained the biggest vaulted structure until St Peter's in Rome, built some 1,000 years later.

The vast volume is based on a transition from a square structure to a circular dome supported on semicircular arches and pendentives between them. The spatial effect on the interior in its 70 metre length and the 31 metre superimposed dome is breathtaking. In 1453, the building became a mosque and in 1935, a museum.

The other landmark structure is the Blue Mosque built 1,000 years later. What Hagia Sophia has on the interior, this building has on its exterior composition. Another architectural highlight is the restored Greek and Roman city of Ephesus, particularly the Library of Celsus. The restoration of its main façade was undertaken by the Austrian Government.

Cappadocia is an area in central Turkey which is in large parts covered with eroded mountains of Tufa, a soft volcanic stone. Over centuries people have carved spaces and caves into these and created virtual cities both inside the mountains and underground. These excavated spaces maintain a constant temperature, enabling people to avoid the extreme climate of the area, intense heat and cold, to live comfortably and to store vegetables and fruit. They create a vast sculpturesque landscape of perforated peaked mountains and valleys.

Istanbul, Hagia Sophia, 6th Century

3

4

2 Istanbul, Mosque of Sultan Ahmed (Blue Mosque), 1606-16

Architect: Mehmet Aga

The forecourt is surrounded by a domed arcade leading into a square structure with heavy supporting piers. Six minarets add to a finely proportioned totality.

3 Istanbul, Hagia Sophia, 6th Century

This enormous church interior with its suspended central dome is a heroic structural feat for its time.

4 Ankara, Memorial to Atatürk, 1944-53

The country's revered leader who "brought Turkey into the 20th Century". A vast ceremonial open space is surrounded by arcades with the stripped classical style mausoleum on its axis.

5

6

7

5, 7 Ephesus, The Library of Celsus, 260 AD

The reconstruction and preservation of the façade were conducted by Prof. Friedmund Hueber of the Austrian Archaeological Institute. Alternating curved and triangular pediments above and flat offset entablatures below are carried by columns, which create a scintillating façade composition.

6 Ephesus

The Roman amphitheatre built into naturally sloping ground.

8 Cappadocia

Entrances to ancient cave dwellings, cut into eroded mountains of soft Tufa, volcanic stone.

Israel

The architecture of Israel can be divided into two parts; the ancient monuments, which are more of religious than architectural interest, and the new architecture in the cities, especially in Tel Aviv, which is a young and rapidly developing metropolis.

The urban plan for Tel Aviv was designed by Sir Patrick Geddes starting in 1931. Speedy development took place following his plan, which coincided with the arrival of German refugee immigrant architects, led by Erich Mendelsohn.

The results are a unique example of a city exclusively of modern architecture and consistent white structures mostly built by architects trained in the tradition of the Bauhaus. Of particular interest are the wide boulevards with central tree-lined pedestrian routes, and separated traffic lanes on either side (such as Rothschild-Avenue). The image of the city is one of a unified architecture of medium height white buildings. Areas of early (50 to 80 year old) structures are now being restored progressively to look as new. The larger recent areas of apartments, city office towers and university buildings are of very high standard.

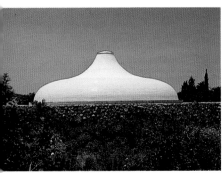

1 Jerusalem
The Jaffa Gate leading to the Old City through the Citadel.

2 Jerusalem, The Israel Museum Shrine of the Books, depository of the Dead Sea Scrolls, 1965
Architects: Friedrich Kiesler and Armand Bartos
The accessible form of the Museum Hall is based on the profile of the ancient container in which the scrolls were found. The arresting sculptural exterior is clad in gloss white ceramics.

3 Jerusalem, The Western or "Wailing Wall", 20 BC
Is a remnant of the temple destroyed in 70 AD. The grand public space in front of the wall is the most revered urban area of the city. The gilded "Dome of Rock" 690 AD is seen in the left background.

4

4 Jerusalem
View from the ramparts surrounding the Old
City with the Citadel's Tower of David.

5 Jerusalem
The Billy Rose sculpture garden in the Israel
Museum. Freestanding screen walls form
an open spatial environment through which
visitors can stroll. The screen walls create a
background for each individual work of art,
without visual distraction.

6 Jerusalem, The Hadassa Hospital, 1939
Architect: Erich Mendelsohn
This excellent facility was built by the emin-
ent and influential German modern architect
who had left Germany in the early 1930s.

Jordan

With a history going back millennia, the country which stretches from the Sea of Galilee in the North, to the Gulf of Aqaba in the South, is a veritable treasure trove of architectural highpoints.

The most spectacular of these is the rose-red ancient city of Petra. Virtually none of it buildings are freestanding, but carved into the face of the rugged sandstone mountains The approach is through a natural gorge more than 1 km long, from 2 metres wide and 200 metres deep. Emerging from this chasm, the first glimpse of the "Treasury" building takes one's breath away. The Roman influence in antiquity is evident in the finely wrought façade-architecture, some of which recalls surprising Baroque characteristics long before its time.

The earliest inhabitants were rock-cave dwellers, and with some spaces in the hollowed-out sandstone were lived-in by nomadic Berbers until recent times.

The remains of the Roman town Jerash, with its curved open forum surrounded by freestanding stone columns is a superb example of Roman town planning.

Crusader strongholds such as Shobak and Ajlun in the North are exceeded in design by the desert castles of Qasar-Kharana and Qusayr Amra, serenely freestanding in the vast expanse of the eastern desert area. Their simple geometric forms and fine ston walls are recognised by UNESCO as World Heritage Sites.

To the South is the dramatic mountainous sandy Wadi-Rum area, the setting of the Lawrence of Arabia film.

1 Petra, Treasury, 1st Century AD
Approached through the Siq, a 1.2 km lon narrow gorge and suddenly coming upon this rock-cut building is the ultimate thrill of discovery for the visitor.

2

3

4

2-4 Ajlun, Ar-Rabad, 1185
The hilltop stone castle near the Jordan
Valley is typical of Islamic military
architecture. Its spaces are connected
by stone vaulted intersecting passages.

5-14 Jerash, 333 BC - 500 AD
The Roman city is entered through
Hadrian's Arch, 129 AD. The oval shaped
forum is defined by freestanding columns,
which are connected at their capitals.

6 Temple of Artemis, 150-170 AD

7 Hadrian's Arch, 129 AD

10 Jerash
The forum's colonnade extends to define
the main streets of the town, lined with
monumental public buildings.

12 The Agora
Surrounding columns and stone benches
create a decorative centre in this market
square.

**13 Nymphaeum, Temple to Artemis,
191 AD**

14 Jerash
The egg and dart stone carving of
a Roman entablature.

5

6

8

10

12

14

15

16

17

15 Shobak, 1115 AD
A fortified hilltop crusader castle, with
a fine silhouette.

16, 17 Qasr-Kharana
Standing alone in a treeless desert area this
impressive building has finely proportioned
exposed stone walls. The internal spaces
face an open central court.

18 Qusayr Amra, 705 AD
The barrel-vaulted structure with domes
and frescoes is influenced by Roman
precedents. It was restored and is now
a UNESCO World Heritage site.

9 Petra Treasury

arved into the rock face on one side of a
earing this edifice creates an unforgettable
nage. The classical Roman façade with its
roken pediment pre-empts Baroque forms
f 1500 years later.

0 Petra Monastery

tanding high on a mountain top, the
ock-cut structure is architecturally
eminiscent to the Treasury, but faces
wide open plateau.

1 Petra

rock-cut tomb.

2-25 Petra

açades of rock-cut buildings surround the
des of Petra's extensive central valley.

20

21

22

23

Of all the cities of what used to be Persia, it is in Isfahan, that Islamic architecture reached its peak in the 16th Century. Located in a seemingly endless expanse of rock and sand, Isfahan lies like a huge oasis with large trees and lush foliage. Emerging from this canopy of vegetation are the inimicable shapes of domes, cupolas and minarets of the city, glistening with brightly coloured geometric patterned ceramic exteriors.

The focal point of the city is the half-kilometre long central square, the Meydan, surrounded by domed structures. At its short end stands the blue Imam Mosque. From its entrance atrium, facing the square, the main building turns at a forty-five degree angle, which creates a strong visual opposition to the rectangular, often water filled reflecting surface of the Meydan.

At the opposite end of the long surface of the square is the gateway to the ancient bazaar with its top lit, vaulted passages filled with shopping stalls.

Isfahan, Imam Mosque, 1612-30
Reflected at the end of the water filled
Meydan focal square of Isfahan.

Isfahan
Plan of the Meydan Square

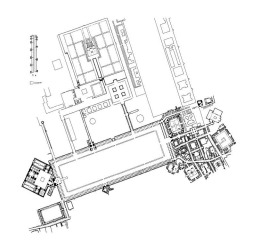

4

3 Isfahan
View on to the Meydan from the roof of a
galleried arcade.

4 Isfahan
Arched decorated entry portico.

6

5 Isfahan
The ancient bazaar, a high, top-lit vaulted structure with stalls lining the criss-crossing passages.

6 Isfahan
The pointed dome and minaret of the Imam Mosque.

7 Isfahan
The Masjit-i-Imam with typical geometric repeated ceramic surfaces, which permit infinite numbers of permutations.

Morocco

Lying between the Mediterranean and the Sahara, the country is traversed by the dramatic Atlas Mountains, snow capped most of the year. Historically inhabited by a resilient Berber population, the country has never been subjugated by numerous invaders.

Of particular architectural interest are the ancient fortified hill-top towns and the villages in valleys of the foothills on both sides of the Atlas Mountains. Built of mud brick walls with flat roofs, they create uniform coloured unique abstract patterns in the mostly dry and barren landscape.

The fortified towns with tall defence towers are the Kasbahs built mostly in the dry river valleys of the Draa and Dades. The best known of these is at Ait Benhaddou, which is a popular movie location.

The cities of Morocco have densely populated centres (the "Medina") with alleys rather than streets barely more than a metre wide. Focal points are the Souq or bazaars, the commercial backbone of the city in which workshops, wool stores and living quarters have not changed in centuries. The uninitiated visitor is easily lost in this labyrinth, lacking any street names.

The imperial cities of Meknes, Fes and Marrakesh have architectural focal points of the surrounding walls with protective towers and the distinctive design of palace and mosques.

1 Taroudant
The town is surrounded by magnificent crenellated red mud walls.

Tioulit
protected town in the Anti-Atlas.

, 4 Dades Valley
ed mud brick villages of the Dades Valley
reate even coloured rectangular abstract
atterns seen against the snow covered
igh Atlas Mountains.

3

4

5

Meknes, The Rouah
uins of the 17th Century royal stables,
hich at one time housed 12,000 horses.

Marrakesh
rotective city walls.

Meknes
etail of the King's palace gates of gold.

6

7

From the early days of European migration to America, in the 17th Century, the building prototype was based on English precedent even if mostly translated into the locally available material in abundance: timber. The predominance of European culture continued and reached a high point under President Thomas Jefferson who was influenced by European classic architecture during his term as America's Ambassador to France. He was a naturally gifted amateur architect, evidenced in his exemplary design for the Campus of the University of Virginia in 1819-26.

American architects in the 19th Century followed the English and French prevalent stylisms until the Industrial Revolution when dramatic advances were made technically and aesthetically. The use of iron enabled buildings to rise higher, aided by the development of the Otis elevator. Economic expansion and consequent wealth allowed architects like Louis Sullivan and Frank Lloyd Wright to unfold their inventive genius of structural daring and a new spaciousness in their buildings. It helped skyscrapers reach unprecedented heights in the early 20th Century.

The 1930s saw the arrival of European émigré architects who could no longer teach or build under the rise of the totalitarian Nazi regime, Walter Gropius who founded the influential Bauhaus, Marcel Breuer, the pioneer of steel furniture, and renowned teacher and designer Mies van der Rohe, its last director, were all invited to teach at Harvard and I.I.T. in Chicago and obtained increasingly important commissions to build. This had immeasurable influence on the young generation and large competing firms of architects such as Skidmore Owings & Merrill. Architecture of high quality reached its zenith in the 1950s and 1970s. Under the pressure toward commercial and advertising newness, "a new architecture every Monday morning", brought style fads into existence, fed by the media who published and listened to influential, articulate but opportunistic practitioners.

The cultural base which brought European Modern Architecture into existence was

issing and was soon replaced with fashions
historistic decorative modes in the 70s
nd 80s, ie. postmodernism, deconstruct-
ism, etc, all meaningless labels coined by
on-practising academics and journalists.
s with all fads, these soon cloyed the
ppetite for "newness" and disappeared.
evertheless, important progressive build-
gs, skyscrapers for successful corporation,
useums, fine houses and interiors mostly
r the wealthy, had been brought into
xistence, by Breuer, Neutra, Mies van der
ohe, Pei, Saarinen, Meier, and the most
rilliant, Frank Lloyd Wright. Le Corbusier
esigned his only U.S. building at Harvard
niversity.
y the end of the 20th Century and the
eath of pioneering architects, a hiatus of
esthetic development gave way to aim-
ssness, fake historicism and a search for
usive convincing directions.
riven mainly by market forces, in contrast
 most European countries, no large scale
wn planning or high quality social housing
ave come into existence in the USA.

1

**1 New York, Rockefeller Center,
1929-40**
*Architects: Reinhard & Hofmeister with
Raymond Hood*
Simultaneously with the Empire State and
the Chrysler Tower, this landmark of New
York was built during the Great Depression.
It consists of nine various height buildings
with the 70-storey RCA Tower its centrepiece. What is admirable in the complex
are the large open pedestrian spaces
which have remained a magnet attracting
people to its malls and plazas.

2

3

2-7 Charlottesville, University of Virginia, 1819-26

Architect: Thomas Jefferson

The symmetrical U-shaped central space terminates in the Roman Pantheon-like library building in this serenely beautiful environment. Five double-storey pavilions connected by low classical colonnades contain teaching and living accommodation. Jefferson was a naturally gifted amateur architect. His direct and ingenious planning was exemplary, not only aesthetically, but by inventive structural devices such as the long and thin self-supporting wave-shaped brick walls achieving much with little effort and material.

9 Chicago, Illinois, Carson Pirie Scott, 1899-1904

Architect: Louis Sullivan
This influential pioneer architect was the first to give expressive strength to early skyscraper buildings which were based on iron skeleton construction. The ground level exterior is encased in cast iron decorative panels, the American counterpart to European art-nouveau of the time.

10 Chicago, The Rookery, 1885-88

Architects: Daniel H. Burnham, John Wellborn Root, Frank Lloyd Wright (reconstruction)
The exposed iron structure supporting the central glazed court's roof is an example of progressive engineering design in the 19th century.

9

10

11

12

13

11, 14 Oak Park, Illinois, Unity Temple, 1904-07

Architect: Frank Lloyd Wright
One of the first "binuclear" or "H plans" later used extensively by others, whereby the main hall and subsidiary spaces are separate and connected with a narrowed entrance link. The powerful solid concrete building has a clear structural expression in the hall, emphasised by the source of daylight. Deep glazed coffers in the roof and horizontal windows placed between the corner supporting elements.

13 Frank Lloyd Wright, 1867-1959

12, 15 Chicago, Illinois, Robie House, 1906-10

Architect: Frank Lloyd Wright
This is one of Wright's most famous works characterised by hugely cantilevered low slung roof planes, interlocking volumes and planes and sweeping horizontals.

16

17

18

19

6 Chicago, Illinois, Crown Hall, I.I.T., 1950-56
Architect: Mies van der Rohe
The main floor of this architecture school consists of a single large space, supported by an external steel frame and enveloped in glass. It is one of Mies' most expressive concepts of a powerful minimal structure.

7 Chicago, Illinois, John Hancock Tower, 1965-70, 1968-75
Architects: Skidmore, Owings & Merrill
The huge tapering tower contains both commercial office space and apartments. The external structural cross bracing gives a distinctive character to the building.

8 Chicago, Federal Center, 1970
Architect: Mies van der Rohe
This typical black framed curtain wall tower is made unique by the placing of the large orange coloured Alexander Calder stabile sculpture.

9 Chicago, Sears Tower, 1974
Architects: Skidmore, Owings & Merrill
Until 1996 it was the tallest building in the world. Its silhouette is made up of a cluster of smaller towers of different heights, generated by the different heights of the groups of elevators.

20

20 Washington DC, Dulles International Airport, 1958-62
Architect: Eero Saarinen
The sweeping catenary roof structure is supported by outward leaning concrete pylons and steel tension cables hung between them, resulting in a huge column-free space.

21 Washington DC, Monument
The focal axis of the capital with its obelisk as seen from the Lincoln Memorial, 1911-1922, Architect Henry Bacon, is based on the Washington Plan by Pierre Charles L'Enfant in 1791.

21

22, 23 Washington DC, East Wing, National Gallery of Art, 1975
Architect: Ieoh Ming Pei
The basis of this superbly designed monumental building is triangular geometry and forms derived from it. The central main space is covered with a glass roof from which a red Alexander Calder mobile sculpture hangs and is kept in constant motion by the ventilation system.

24 Ieoh Ming Pei, *1917

25 New Harmony, Indiana, The Atheneum, 1975-79
Architect: Richard Meier
Built in a historic town founded by a Utopian community in 1815, this is a centre for visitors' orientation and community cultural events. The elaborate spatial complex contains exhibition areas and an auditorium all connected by internal access ramps. The generous glass areas allow views over the lushly planted surroundings and the nearby Wabash River.

24

26

27

26, 27 Collegeville, Minn., St John's Abbey and University, 1953-70
Architect: Marcel Breuer
The folded concrete Abbey Church is supported by ground level columns with glass walls between that admit daylight to the monumental interior which is tapered both vertically and horizontally. The dramatic freestanding bell banner straddles the entrance.

28, 29 Muskegon, Mich., St Francis de Sales Church, 1961-67
Architect: Marcel Breuer
Rising from a rectangular plan at the ground, three trapezoidal planes form the front and rear walls and the roof. Two twisting hyperbolic paraboloid side walls complete the enclosure. The unique interior contains a freestanding balcony.

30 Marcel Breuer, 1902-1981

30

31

31, 32 Syracuse, NY, Everson Museum, 1968

Architect: Ieoh Ming Pei

The contrast between the minimalist rectilinear sculptural exterior and the interior could not be greater. The flying cantilevers outside give way to constantly changing spatial excitements inside. The main space is traversed by a curvilinear stair and ramp with linear sources of daylight.

32

33

34

33, 34 Fort Worth, Texas, Kimbell Museum of Art, 1972
Architect: Louis Kahn
Composed of six parallel concrete vaults which span the whole length of the structure, the "servant" spaces between them allowed variations of displays between the top lit galleries within the long vaults.

35 Bear Run, Pennsylvania, Fallingwater, Kaufmann House 1936
Architect: Frank Lloyd Wright
This is Wright's world-famous house, cantilevered over a gushing waterfall in the most beautiful wild natural setting. The vertical rough stone piers support daringly hovering horizontal concrete elements of terraces and suspended spaces. Even though romantic in character, the off-white house is clearly influenced by European modern architecture of the time.

36 San Francisco Houses
These vernacular 19th Century houses with carved timber decorations give whole districts of the city their unmistakable character.

37 San Francisco, Cal., Office Building, 1890
An early steel framed city building with a glass curtain wall façade, long before this was re-introduced by European émigré architects, 50 years later.

38 San Francisco, Cal., Russell Residence, 1948
Architect: Erich Mendelsohn
One of the few American buildings by Mendelsohn, this lavish residence is built overlooking an expansive public park.

39 Oakland, Cal., Oakland Museum, 1961
Architect: Kevin Roche
The museum consists of low pavilions, connected by landscaped roofs which create the impression of a large stepped park.

40 San Francisco, Cal., Crown Zellerbach Building, 1957
Architect: Skidmore, Owings & Merrill
This office tower is freestanding in landscaped grounds. A circular low bank building with a folded plate roof creates a focus for occupants looking down.

41

41 Los Angeles, Cal., Lovell House, 1928

Architect: Richard Neutra

This well-known house is one of the first examples of uncompromising modern architecture in America. Its light steel frame construction and multi-level spacious interiors influenced much later design in the U.S. and Europe.

42

42 Palm Springs, Cal., Kaufmann House, 1946

Architect: Richard Neutra

Based on a pin-wheel plan, the different wings allow individual panoramic views of the surrounding mountains and desert scenery to every room.

43 Los Angeles, Cal., Charles Ennis House, 1924

Architect: Frank Lloyd Wright

This hillside house, built of decorated cast concrete blocks, recalls Mayan stone carved architecture.

43

44-46 Los Angeles, Cal., The Paul Getty Center and Museum, 1984-97

Architect: Richard Meier

Located on a hilltop above the city, this complex of buildings is the most elaborate anywhere dedicated to art. The various pavilions contain study centres and museums, grouped around large open spaces with gardens, fountains and restaurants. Most buildings are clad in white metal, but some are of split travertine stone resulting in deeply textured surfaces under strong sunlight.

47

47 Boston, Mass., Quincy Market, 1976
Architect: Ben Thompson
This successful urban renewal project
revitalises an early 19th Century market and
warehouse area (designed by Alexander
Parris).

48, 50, 51 Lincoln, Mass., Walter Gropius House, 1937
Architects: Walter Gropius & Marcel Breuer
This revolutionary house is the first work
by these two recently appointed influential
Harvard Professors. The simple rectilinear
outline of the building is sculpted with
hollowed out, recessed spaces, stone
walls and screens. The angled entrance
is recalled in an opposing slanting wall in
the living area.
Other than in books, it is the first deeply
impressive masterpiece of modern
architecture that Gropius' students have
seen (including myself).
Photo 50, the 1946 photo is the earliest
taken, in this book.

48

49

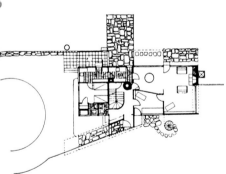
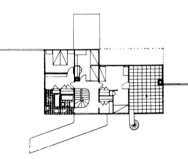

49 Cohasset, Mass., Hagerty House, 1938

Architects: Walter Gropius, Marcel Breuer
The entrance side of the seaside villa faces the ocean on the other side with large areas of glass. The two sides are joined by the open ground space under the suspended part of the house. The resulting landscaped open area is enclosed with stone walls.

52

53

2, 53 New Canaan, Conn., Glass House, 1949

Architect: Philip Johnson

On a visit in 1955, Marcel Breuer (see photo) took me to see this steel framed glass pavilion. It was the first of such totally glazed houses in the USA. It is built in an extensive park-like setting and was later joined by other small buildings, a sculpture pavilion, an underground museum and a guest house.

Mies van der Rohe had sketched such a glass house in 1934 and built the elegant Farnsworth House in Plano, Ill. in 1951.

54

54, 55 Boston, Mass., Museum of Fine Arts, 1981

Architect: Ieoh Ming Pei

This stone clad addition to the large existing museum complex has a central glass vaulted spine from which exhibition spaces emanate horizontally and vertically.

55

56, 57 Cambridge, Mass., Carpenter Center for the Visual Arts, 1963

Architect: Le Corbusier

Built at Harvard University, this is Le Corbusier's only building in North America. Studio spaces are located on either side of a flowing access ramp which penetrates the building and connects two parallel streets. Activities in the studios are visible to all who pass through the building. The south facing spaces are equipped with external sun louvres which add texture to the off-form concrete building. The Center is one of Le Corbusier's most stunning, sculpturally and constructionally. It is also the best maintained of all his buildings.

56

57

8 Manhattan, New York, Wall Street
he financial business district's very narrow
treets are lined with skyscrapers dating
om the early 20th Century. The high rise
uildings dwarf the church tower which
as once a tall landmark.

**9 New York, George Washington
ridge**
his advanced engineering feat of a steel
uspension bridge across the Hudson River
as built in the 1930s. When Mies van der
ohe was interviewed in 1957 and asked
hat he considered the best building in
ew York, he named this bridge.
his photo was taken in 1946 by stopping
e car on the bridge and climbing onto the
otpath!

59

60

61

60, 61 New York, Museum of Modern Art, 1939

Architects: Philip Goodwin & Edward Durre Stone

This culturally important museum started a a plain translucent stone fronted structure. It has undergone many alterations and additions over the years, the best of which is the fine sculpture garden by Philip Johnson.

62, 63, 64 New York, Solomon R. Guggenheim Museum, 1959

Architect: Frank Lloyd Wright

Wright's most celebrated building is based on an extraordinary concept, some 15 years in development. The central top lit atrium is surrounded by spiral gallery spaces, which were much criticised due to the sloping floors and limited ceiling height. With the completion of Wright's original rectilinear wing, with high spaces (Architect C. Gwathmey) the museum functions well and is more popular than ever.

THE SOLOMON R GUGGENHEIM MUSEUM

65

65, 67 New York, Whitney Museum of American Art, 1966

Architect: Marcel Breuer

Placed on a small corner site, the grey granite clad square building steps out toward the top to leave space for an outdoor sculpture court below street level. Unique trapezoidal windows admit daylight to the gallery floors. The beautiful Alexander Calder exhibition in 1976 shows the success of the flexible display lighting from the squared concrete grid ceiling.

66, 68 New York, Seagram Building, 1958

Architect: Ludwig Mies van der Rohe

Mies' masterpiece is recognised as the quintessential skyscraper of the 20th Century. The tower is set back from Park Avenue, creating a public space, on which huge sculptures are often displayed. The minimalist "almost nothing" design of the tower asserts its monumentality and longevity by being clad in bronze. Even wall-wash lighting, developed for the building by Richard Kelly, was used for the first time on the high travertine clad entrance walls.

428

69

70

71

72

9 New York, United Nations Development, 1969

Architect: Kevin Roche
An early example of tower architecture abandoning a routine rectilinear silhouette.

0, 73 New York, Chase Manhattan Bank, 1957-60

Architects: Skidmore, Owings & Merrill (Gordon Bunshaft)
The architecture of this quality headquarters office building offers a neutral background, but gains stature by the placement of major sculptures at ground level by Dubuffet, and in a sunken court by Noguchi.
The Head of the Bank, David Rockefeller's office continues this theme; elegant minimalism, enriched with large colourful artworks.

1, 72 New York, The Ford Foundation, 968

Architects: Eero Saarinen & Kevin Roche
This headquarters building maximises the opportunity offered by its site adjacent to a park. The central high atrium is overlooked from the L-shaped office floors and faces the other two full height glass walls toward the park. High Eucalyptus Trees in the atrium extends the park inside.

73

74 World Trade Center Towers, 1966-7∶

Architect: Minoru Yamasaki

For some 30 years the 100-storey twin office towers were the most visible landmarks of Manhattan. On September 11, 2001, they were destroyed in a terrorist attack by jet aircraft being driven into their sides, causing an inferno, which killed some 3,000 people.

The world asked - how could this have happened?

When visiting the buildings during construction in 1970, I remember being amazed at the exclusive use of lightweight building materials. Their steel structure consisted of closely spaced exterior columns and 20 m floor beams spanning to the elevator core. No concrete was used around firestairs or elevator shafts, instead layers of plasterboard were chosen.

The immense heat generated by the impact explosion of jet fuel weakened the steel structure to such an extent that it caused the progressive collapse of both towers in a short time.

Nevertheless, the structural steel design of the buildings is ingenious and given normal usage would have lasted indefinitely, excluding such an outrageous terrorist attack.

However, my contention is that concrete buildings would have been damaged by the impact, but would not have collapsed.

Canada

There are many fine 19th century public buildings and modern city towers in Canada, mostly adhering to American prototypes in the large cities of Toronto and Montreal. There is however a distinct French influence historically in Eastern Canada, particularly Quebec City. The only time I spent there was during World War II, without opportunities to take photographs, as I was behind barbed wire as an 'enemy alien' internee. In recent years I did visit an outstanding building at the University of British Columbia in Vancouver.

1, 2 Vancouver, Museum of Anthropology, 1976
Architect: Arthur Erickson
Based on local timber tradition, the concrete structure consists of post and beam vertical frame members connected with glass wall and roof infills. The dramatic naturally lit interiors allow for an unusually fine display of the museums collections.

1

Mexico

Mexico has been the home of numerous civilisations for over 3000 years. The Pre-Hispanic cultures had reached a high leve when they were destroyed by the Spanish conquistadores in only a few years. Christianity was imposed on the populatic and left some fine 16th and 17th Century European architecture, especially the ston churches, palaces and public buildings in the cities. Spanish in origin, their modifi-cations even extend the European original with highly decorated gilded interiors and alters.

What I find to be the most remarkable and memorable is the ancient Mayan arch tecture around Oaxaca and on the Yucata peninsula in such centres as Uxmal and Chichen Itza. The planning and compo-sitions of the structures that remain seem to generate a particular affinity to our own time's visual concerns.

The buildings and monuments have beau fully proportioned openings and simple façades of minimal outline which are covered, in controlled areas only, with geometric stone carvings. The steeply sloping pyramids and their relationship to the long rectangular structures continue these compositions in their site placement Mexico's modern architecture is different t contemporary American or European worl which is particularly evident in the work of Luis Barragán and Ricardo Legorreta. The large scale and unadorned dramatically coloured wall surfaces seem to recall the country's ancient buildings.

Uxmal, The Ruler's Palace, 600-900 AD
The stone carved building is in the Mayan Puuc style.

Mitla
14th Century Zapotec recessed stone carved opposing patterns.

Chichén Itzá, Pyrámide de Kukulkan, 800 AD
A fine geometric silhouette stone building is of Mayan religious significance with sacred vault spaces within.

1

4

4-7 Chichén Itzá, 1000 AD

Surrounding stone buildings are seen from
the top of the Pyramid; the long parallel
walls of a ball court with projecting stone
"goal" rings and the "Temple of the
Warriors" with a remaining group of a
Thousand stone columns.

7

8

9

10

1

-11 Uxmal, 600-900 AD

he well preserved stone buildings are of
most impressive architectural design. The
ite planning and disposition of the
tructures create admirable spaces and
istas between them.

12

12-15 Uxmal, 600-900 AD

Grouped around a central pyramid are long structures arranged to form large open courtyards between them. The placement of openings in the façades and particularly the design and proportions of the sculpted stone surfaces are some of the most memorable in Mexico.

3

4

5

16

16-18 Sayil, El Palacio

The only three-tiered Mayan building has an 85 metre long façade decorated with grouped columns and sculpted friezes of masks. The Mayans did not know arch construction, evidenced by the collapse of the outer portion of the steeply stepped stone ground level galleries.

17

18

19 Dzibilchaltun

The 130 metre long palace entry steps
are in fine condition, for their over 1000
year life. The Danish architect, Jørn Utzon,
cites them as his inspiration for the wide
entrance stairs to the Sydney Opera
House.

20 Teotihuacan, 150-600 AD

The site for this ancient Aztec city is
50 km north of Mexico City. It was once
the capital of Mexico's largest Pre-Hispanic
empire. The focal structures in this vast
linear development are two pyramids, the
largest 70 metres high, is dedicated to
the sun, the smaller to the moon. The
surrounding stepped structures were once
colourfully painted.

21

21 Mexico City, Palacio Nacional, 16th Century

The long beautiful façade of this focal building of the Mexican Government takes up one side of the Zocalo. It contains dramatic murals by Diego Rivera (photo taken in 1948).

22 Mexico City, Metropolitan Cathedral, 16th Century

The highly decorated and gilded recessed interior space of the altar is reminiscent of Spanish church architecture of the time.

23-25 Mexico City, Anthropological Museum, 1964
Architect: Pedro Ramírez Vazquez
The large complex of exhibition wings creates an open plaza with a huge umbrella-like fountain supported by only one column. The excellent exhibits depict Mexico's history with models of ancient Aztec cities and carved façades.

26

27

**6, 28 Mexico City, San Cristobal Stable
nd House, 1968**
rchitect: Luis Barragán
his large complex of brilliantly coloured
eestanding pavilions, house, stables
nd screen walls, create a rich spatial-
culptured totality. A pond and gushing
ountain are in the exercise yard for the
wners' thoroughbred horses.

**7 Mexico City, Luis Barragán's Own
louse, 1947**
his unassuming modest house of the
rchitect is full of surprises in the complex
iterior spaces and their natural light
ources. The library's minimal composition
as an open timber stair reaching the upper
oor between two opposing white walls.

28

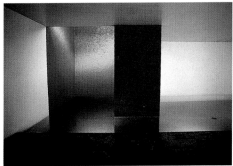

**9 Mexico City, Casa Gilardi Indoor
wimming Pool, 1978**
rchitect: Luis Barragán
he pool is composed of blue, red and
·hite smooth and textured wall and
olumn surfaces. The colours change
·ith the ripple of the water and create an
nexpected translucence. To the user it
lust be a swimming experience through
work of art.

29

0 Luis Barragán, 1902-1988

30

31 Mexico City, San Angel Casa Prieto Lopez, 1950

Architect: Luis Barragán
This house has a typical Mexican entry courtyard surrounded by brightly coloured walls. The inside spaces interact beautifully with large single pane windows opening onto tranquil gardens.

32 Mexico City, Olympic Sports Palast, 1958

Engineer: Felix Candela
The ingenious space frame structure expresses its triangulated protruding elements, which results in a uniquely sculptural exterior.

33 Mexico City, Centro National de las Artes, 1994

Architect: Ricardo Legorreta
The access stair, leading to the buildings of the centre, is typical of Mexican modern architecture which uses brilliant coloured walls.

Peru

The truly outstanding and memorable site in Peru is the "Lost City of the Incas", Machu Picchu, which the marauding Spanish Conquistadores never discovered. Located some 2400 metres high up in the Andes it straddles a mountainside in a spectacular setting.

It was inhabited from the 14th to 16th Centuries by a particularly constructive Pre-Hispanic Andean society that left evidence of their aesthetic creativity. Machu Picchu was home to some 1,000 to 2,000 people, who created an amazing environment of a city meticulously planned and built to incorporate housing and agri-cultural terraces. Public open spaces and long flights of stairs connect different districts.

Culminating in the high up "Temple of the Sun" the entirety is like an enormous sculpture consisting of man-made and natural elements in a particularly sympathetic relationship.

The capital city of the area, Cuzco, gives evidence of its Inca origins by its stone ruins and the Spanish colonial architecture. On the outskirts of town are the remains of a fort, built of cut-stone blocks fitted together so perfectly that no mortar was required. The interlocking irregular shapes of the enormous blocks preserved the walls for centuries, even though the area is known for frequent earthquakes.

Cuzco, Cathedral
The focal point of the city's central square
is a fine piece of 16th Century Spanish
Baroque architecture with elaborate pure
gold interior decorations.

3

4

2-4 Machu Picchu
The Inca city high up in the Andes Mountains with houses and agricultural terraces ingeniously connected by long flights of stone steps.

5 Cuzco
Inca fortification walls of tightly fitted blocks of stone which have resisted earthquakes due to their interlocking shapes.

Argentina

Argentina is symbolised by its capital, Buenos Aires, which is rightly referred to as the "Paris of South America", a city that has a strong European feeling in its architecture and planning. In the early years of the 20th Century the wealth of the country was evidenced by the extravagant public buildings, squares, its opera house and the extraordinary high-rise apartment towers that line the big avenues and express a strong Latin flair in their architecture, combining classical stylism with uniquely exuberant cornices and domed tops.

The huge scale of the city is particularly evidenced by Avenue 9 de Julio, said to be the widest street in the world, with its centrally placed obelisk and eight traffic lanes on each side.

In total contrast to the monumental structures of the city, the La Boca area on the waterfront has small tin clad houses painted in all colours of the rainbow. In the nearby town of La Plata, Le Corbusier designed a house and office for a doctor, overlooking a park. Supported by a grid of circular pilotis, the surgery facing the street and the house at the rear are connected by ramps cutting through between the two separate structures, which generate fascinating outdoor/indoor spatial effects.

1 Buenos Aires, Plaza de Mayo
The large civic square of the city used for public celebrations and demonstrations is lined with important buildings including the impressive Casa Rosada, the President's Palace.

3

4

2 Buenos Aires
The typical elaborately decorated high-rise apartment towers from the time when Argentina was one of the wealthiest countries in the world.

3 Buenos Aires, La Boca
The colourful district of tin-clad buildings near the waterfront.

4 Le Plata, Dr Currutchet House, 1949
Architect: Le Corbusier
Le Corbusier's only building in Argentina. The separated surgery and house wings are intertwined with intriguing spatial effects.

Brazil

The Portuguese architectural influence was paramount during the colonial days of the country from the 16th to the 19th Century. The historically protected cities such as Ouro Preto are rich in fine 17th Century Baroque churches. Although these are mostly well protected and worth visiting, the architectural focus of Brazil is in its modern architecture. This is what I was determined to experience during my stay there on route in 1948. During three months working with Oscar Niemeyer, the dramatic developments of his archi-tecture had a lasting affect on me. At that time, soon after World War II, there was virtually no comparable modern architecture in the USA and buildings such as the new Ministry of Education in Rio were over-whelmingly convincing as the appropriate architecture for our time.

Gropius, in his writings, referred to Niemeyer rather disparagingly as the Paradiesvogel (Bird of Paradise) of architecture. The huge number of his completed buildings has a certain flamboyance and curvilinearity in common, which recall the qualities of Brazil colonial Baroque period. Undoubtedly influenced by Le Corbusier (who visited Brazil in the 1930s) in the essentials of planning and structure, Niemeyer's work has a disarming directness and clarity of concept that is raised to the level of a unique art form. His appointment to design a new capital city of Brazil led to an unsur passed large scale planning solution (in collaboration with Lucio Costa) and group ings of buildings without equal. As an example, there is no need for, nor were any traffic lights planned in this city where the ingenious road system makes these redundant.

One of his latest works (at age over 90!) is the Museum in Niteroi. This daring concept and structure is beyond belief or descript-ion. After a visit one feels confident that there is hope for our time, that architecture will develop into an art form that can take its place alongside the finest man has ever built in the past.

Rio de Janeiro, Copacabana
his is part of one of the most beautiful
ities in the world. Copacabana is the
est known of several beachfronts with its
reat sweep of a sandy beach edged by
parallel row of tall buildings. Steep, bare
ranite mountains such as the "Sugarloaf",
orm the dramatic background.

Drawing by Oscar Niemeyer,
haracteristic of his flamboyant curvilinear
rchitecture.

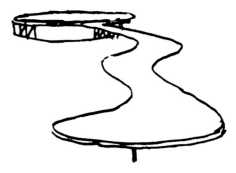

5 Rio de Janeiro, Ministry of Education, 1941

Architects: Le Corbusier, Oscar Niemeyer and others

This pioneering structure demonstrates the effective use of adjustable horizontal louvre sun protection on its fully glazed northern façade. The 10 m high open ground level portico is adorned with a tile (Azulejos) mural by Portinari.

Oscar Niemeyer, *1907

4

5

6

7

8

7-10 Pampulha, Mina Gerais, Recreational Buildings and a Church built around a Lake, 1943

Architect: Oscar Niemeyer
Near Bello Horizonte, the capital of the State of Minas Gerais, a restaurant, yacht club, a church (with a tile mural by Portinari) and a casino, were built on the shore of an artificial lake. They represent a display of mature modern Brazilian architecture by Niemeyer.

11 Brasilia, The Capital, 1957-60

Architect: Oscar Niemeyer
This focal point of Brazil's new capital places the two national Congress chambers on a platform. Their opposing convex and concave circular forms with the dual administrative towers between them, result in the iconical silhouette of the city.

12

13

14

12-14 São Paulo, Memorial of the Latin American States, 1990

Architect: Oscar Niemeyer

The large urban site contains an assembly plaza with a symbolically bleeding open hand sculpture by Niemeyer. Crisp white freestanding buildings surround the space. Their long span concrete structures create an interactive sculptural totality.

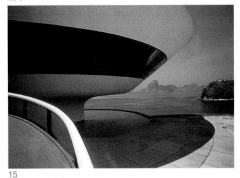

15

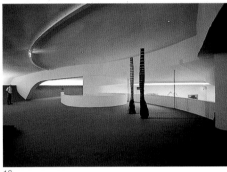

16

15-18 Niteroi, Contemporary Art Museum, 1996
Architect: Oscar Niemeyer
Built on a peninsular reaching into Rio's harbour, the form and structure of this incredible building borders on the unbelievable. Prestressed radial interior ribs emanate from its central supporting hollow ring column. The upward sweep of the mushroom shaped glazed exterior wall runs parallel to the 'Sugarloaf' mountain in the distance.

19 São Paulo, Copan Building, 1951
Architect: Oscar Niemeyer
This co-operative apartment building takes on a wave-shaped plan form to fit onto the irregular inner city site. Two continuous horizontal louvres to each floor act as effective sun protection and afford privacy to the inhabitants.

Japan

The architecture of Japan was influenced historically by Chinese building practice, although many differences developed. Japan's humid and warm summer climate as well as frequent earthquakes resulted in lightweight timber buildings raised off the ground that are resistant to earth tremors. The visual simplicity of important palace structures has had an influence on western architecture in the 20th Century. Elegant refinement and minimalist austere open interconnected spaces have influenced the modern architecture in much of the world exemplified by the work of Mies van der Rohe. Some of Frank Lloyd Wright's work has been influenced by Japan and conversely his multi-level entrance spaces in the Imperial Hotel in Tokyo has had an effect on modern Japanese architecture. Some parts of the lobby space have been reconstructed elsewhere in Japan after the Hotel's demolition in 1960.

After World War II great strides were made in modern Japanese architecture, not only in advanced technology, allowing earthquake resistant tall buildings, but expressing and infusing characteristics of traditional Japanese architecture in modern buildings.

The relationship between the restrained formal geometries of Japanese interiors is brought into a particular refined fusion with its landscape and garden architecture.

A romantically peaceful serenity results.

2 Kyoto, Katsura Palace, 1620-62
Architect: Kobori Enshu

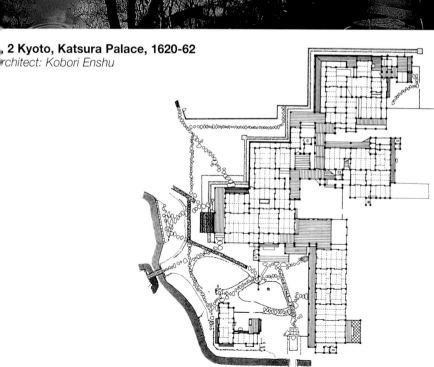

4

5

3-5 Kyoto, Katsura Palace, 1663
Architect: Kobori Enshu

The masterpiece of serene simplicity is set in harmony with a picturesque landscape environment. The restrained minimalism of the timber building consists only of supporting columns and an open planned interior which can be subdivided, opened or closed to the outside with their sliding panels, to serve diverse uses.

The garden surroundings are contrived to idealise nature and brings water, stepping stones, paths and plants into a romantic scene of perfection.

The unornamented interiors are devoid of western furniture, with a bare geometric order created by the use of multiple tatami rice-straw floor mats.

6

7

6, 7 Kyoto, Shishinden Imperial Palace, rebuilt 1855

The dominant concave roof covers a structure of equally spaced columns. Although the building is centuries old it is repaired and rebuilt periodically, seen in the façade of adjacent old and new timber columns.

8 Kyoto, The Golden Pavilion, 1397, rebuilt 1950s

The gilded shrine is built in a park surrounded by water. It exudes an atmosphere of untouchable perfection.

9

10

9 Kyoto, Heian Shrine, 1882
The large overhanging roof and widely
spaced columns mark the entrance to
a series of courtyards within.

10, 12 Yokohama, Imperial Villa,
straddling a stream.
The weathered timber old garden court
entrance gate.

11 Kyoto
A typical pagoda, a religious structure, was
built following Chinese historic origins.

13

14

15

13-15 Tokyo, The Imperial Hotel, 1916-1922 (demolished 1967)

Architect: Frank Lloyd Wright

Penelope and I stayed in the hotel just before its demolition. All interiors and furniture, designed by Wright, were still intact. The entrance hall was the most remarkable space in the huge complex. It had seven different levels, interacting spatially and all merging into the entrance foyer.

Built of brick and carved lava stone, the structure was supported on an ingenious system of driven piles, which saved the building in the disastrous 1923 earthquake.

16

16-18 Tokyo, Olympic Pool, 1964
Architect: Kenzo Tange
A unique structure of only two concrete
supports and a prestressed steel net
covering the concave roof.

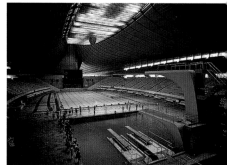

17

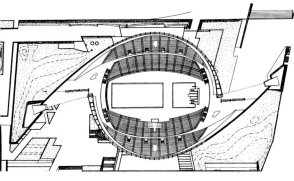

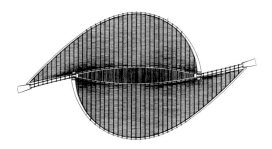

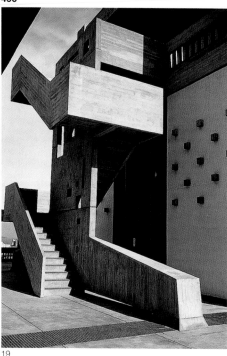

19

19, 20 Takamatsu, Kagawa Prefecture, 1955-58

Architect: Kenzo Tange

Solidly built of exposed textured concrete, the modern office building recalls traditional Japanese ponds with sculptural stone blocks.

The projecting concrete floor beams are reminiscent of early timber structures.

China

This ancient land enjoys a long history and great achievements with many architectural miracles such as "The Great Wall", built to protect the northern borders from predatory mountain people of the Steppes. The 6000 km long structure contains guard towers and Garrison towns. It is said to be the only man-made structure that is visible from the moon.

"The Forbidden City" contains the most impressive series of monumental structures interspersed with large courtyards connected by white marble stairs. The entry court is traversed by a wave shaped watercourse which generates a unique atmosphere in the vast open space.

, 2 Beijing, Great Wall of China

uccessive emperors ordered The Great
Wall of China to be constructed, protecting
he country from Northern Incursions. The
wall was started between the seventh to
he fifth centuries B.C. and was continu-
usly strengthened over the ages to
ecome 7m high and wide, built on
n internal earth core, faced with brick
xteriors on a stone base. The huge wall,
ome 6000 km long, winds up and down
cross the mountainous landscape. Its
cale is unparalleled in the architecture of
ortifications.

3

4

8 Beijing, The Forbidden City, 1403-20

This imperial palace housed the emperors from the 14th until the early 20th centuries and consists of a virtual city with halls, pavilions and towers covering a walled compound of some 720,000 square metres, which takes more than half an hour to traverse. Buildings face a series of large courtyards interrupted by temple structures, residence halls and religious shrines. On my second visit, in 1977, new snow fell at night and offered a unique view of the first snow covered large court, the only space containing a curvilinear watercourse and stone foot bridges.

5

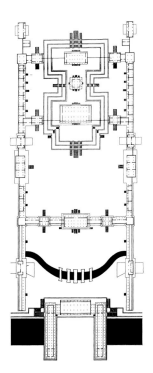

6

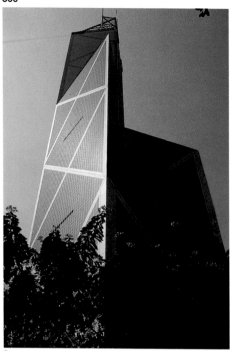

9

9 Hong Kong, Bank of China Tower, 1982-90

Architect: Ieoh Ming Pei
This landmark of the city has a triangulated exposed steel frame which expresses the three dimensional form of the structure.

10, 11 Beijing, Temple of Heaven

The colourful carved timber ceiling structure of the circular Temple of Heaven shrine.

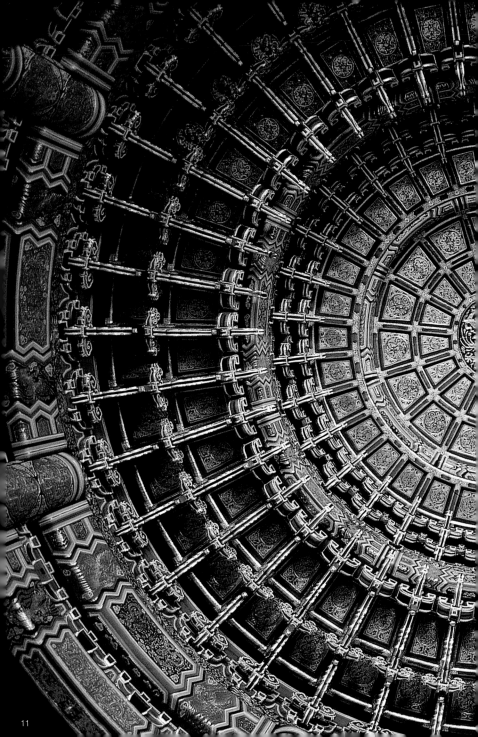

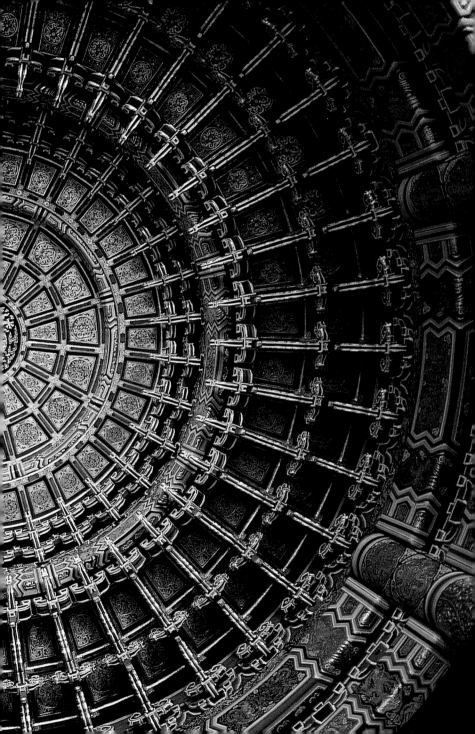

Indonesia

Java, the central island of Indonesia, is the most architecturally fascinating and populous in the country of over 200 million people It contains the finest remaining Hindu and Buddhist temple architecture of the seventh and 10th centuries.

Of the world's active volcanoes, 34% are in Indonesia. In the central area where once stood 240 temples most have collapsed. Reconstruction of them have been in progress since the 1930s.

1 Java, Parambanan

-4 Java, Parambanan

he progress of restoring and rebuilding the
emples in central Java is a slow task, that
as lasted for decades and is still continu-
ng. The blocks of dark volcanic stone have
een collected and assembled with a num-
er of temples completed. They are solid
all structures, only covered on the outside
vith decorative elaborate carvings and
gures reusing the scattered stone blocks.
tanding in the open landscape the visual
npact of these monolithic tower structures
powerful.

3

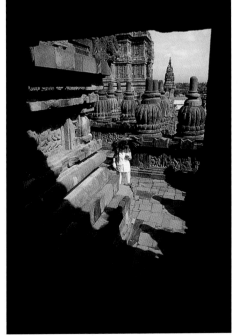

4

5

6

5-8 Java, Borobudur

The most memorable of temples is the terraced solid stone square pyramid, with statues, relief carvings and "stupas" rising along continuously winding terraces and steep steps to the 34 metre high roof. The tallest inverted, 8 metre high stupa forms the top and is ringed with smaller perforated, inverted bell-like enclosures, each with a different gesture, sitting Buddha sculpture contained within.

India

The enduring achievements of Indian civilisation lie in its architecture. Built during the rule of various dominant cultures, Persian, Indian and Mughal styles merge in building of great refinements. These were often built centuries apart such as palaces, temples, forts, tombs, astrological observation structures and expansive town planning schemes. The most memorable of these were built during the powerful Mughal Empire in the 16th Century, mainly located in northern India's Rajasthan, in Delhi and Agra.

The British influence in the 19th Century produced grandiose government buildings Mumbai (Bombay) remains today the pre-eminent Victorian gothic city in the world. New Delhi was created as India's capital city by Lutyens in 1912 and was built in a hybrid of European and Indian architectural modes.

In the early 1950s Le Corbusier was invited to undertake the planning and building of a huge new city, Chandigarh, in the Punjab, which had lost its capital, Lahore, during partition.

This immense undertaking can be compared to Brazil's capital Brasilia, both the successful totally planned new cities of the 20th Century and both created by two of the era's greatest architects.

1 Agra Fort, Khass Mahal, 1565
This white marble pavilion housed the private apartments of the Emperor.

2

3

4

Agra, Taj Mahal
The detailed entry shows dark stone inlaid surfaces in the white marble exterior.

4 Agra Fort
Carved marble surrounds the pool and scalloped arches support the pavilion.

Agra Fort
View from Agra Fort toward the Taj Mahal in the distance.

Agra, Taj Mahal, 1631-1657
Architect: Isa Khan
The mausoleum was constructed by Emperor Shah Jahan in memory of his deceased wife.
This world famous white marble iconic building has a graceful composition, arrangement of a central dome, towers and pointed arches, all raised on a podium and focused on an axial reflecting water-course.

Agra, Itimad Ud Daulah (The Small Taj), 1622-1628
This is the first white marble temple built with inlaid precious stones, foreshadowing the Taj Mahal, a building using beautiful geometric proportions and perforated stone grille exteriors.

5

8

9

10

11

8-10 New Delhi, Parliamentary Compound, 1912-30

Architects: Lutyens and Baker

A grand axial boulevard focuses on the domed Vice Regal Palace's formal gate, leading to the sumptuous multi-winged establishment.

Flanking both sides of the approach are government offices that have characteristic Indian Chattri pavilion projections with parasol shaped domed roofs.

The circular Parliament House, designed by Baker in 1930, is surrounded by a recessed colonnade above a solid stone base.

The atmosphere of this central government area is a grandiose imperial gesture, the final stage of the British Empire's rule in India.

11, 12 Jaipur, Hawa Mahal (Palace of the Winds), 1799

Architect: Maharaja Pratap Singh II

Jaipur's landmark is only a façade through which the city's main street can be over-looked with projecting honeycombed sandstone bays and half Chattri domed roofs.

13 Jaipur, Jantar Mantar (or Observatory), 1728

4-16 Jaipur, Jantar Mantar (or Observatory), 1728

Jantar Mantar was the Rajput Jai Singh's passion for astronomy. Covering a large open area are sculpture like structures from which positions of stars, altitudes and azimuths can be observed and eclipses calculated.

17, 18 Jaipur, City Palace, 18th Century

Located in the heart of the old city, a series of arched entries lead to courtyards, gardens and inner buildings, all with typical overhanging thin edged cornices and perforated stone screen façade infills.

15

16

17

18

19

20

19-21 Udaipur, Lake Palace, by Maharana Jagat Singh II, 1754

Located in the centre of Udaipur and built on an island in the lake, this formal royal palace must be the most romantic, superbly crafted and extravagant creation anywhere. Surrounded by stone arched pavilions facing the water, its central courtyards are filled with lotus ponds and swimming pools. The palace is now used as a luxury hotel.

22

22-30 Fatehpur Sikri, 1571-85
Capital of the Mughal Empire, Emperor
Akbar. This is among the finest cities built
by edict of an Indian Emperor in the 16th
Century. The interlocking layout of various
size open spaces, watercourses, ringed
and punctuated by freestanding skilfully
positioned structures, all provide constantly
changing vistas as one strides through
this amazing city. Built of durable red
sandstone, some opposing white marble
pavilions, perforated screens and fine
workmanship, it is still something of a
mystery why it was deserted so soon
after its completion. The only explanation
offered is the problem of water supply for
its population. This cohesive complex
creates a beautiful totality without equal.

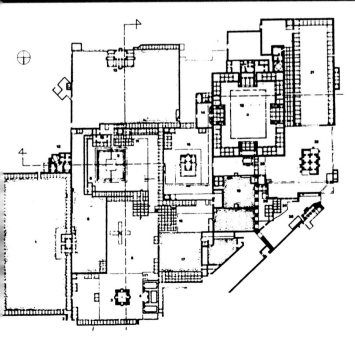

27

28

31 Chandigarh, 1950-1985

Architect: Le Corbusier

The plan of the capital to the north of the
city shows the High Court, the Parliament
and the Secretariat with the open hand
sculpture and the Governor's palace to be
built later.

The housing districts for 150,000 people
was to be enlarged to 500,000 inhabitants.

32 Chandigarh

The Secretariat during construction, on
my first visit when I met Le Corbusier in
Chandigarh, in 1955. The towers attached
to the slab building contained access
ramps used for women labourers carrying
up buckets of concrete. The entire city was
built by hand.

33 Chandigarh

The Parliament building seen with the
foothills of the Himalayas in the distance.
The two chambers of government are in
the centre of the building, projecting far
above the roof and surrounded by circu-
lation space.

Offices are planned against the exterior
walls, covered with sun protection blades.

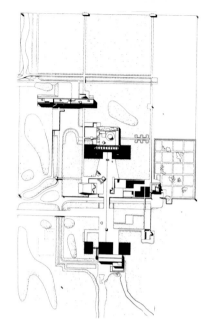

31

34

35

4-36 Chandigarh, The Parliament Building

The dramatically upswept portico of the main entrance, with the Secretariat in the background, both reflect in the large water basins. The plan and cross section show the top lit continuously changing inner space around the chambers, which is the most beautiful of any of Le Corbusier's interiors.

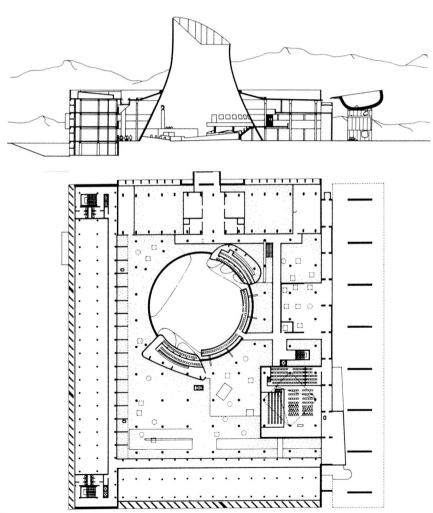

37, 38, 40 Chandigarh
The Secretariat building is 254 meters long and 42 meters high, with the ramped pedestrian access tower projecting from the façade. The continuous repetitive sun protected office galleries are interrupted by irregular height ministerial offices and formal meeting spaces, all of which, including the office's proportions, are based on Le Corbusier's modular system.

39, 41 Chandigarh
The High Court building has an arched parasol-like roof structure which together with the brise-soliel along the ground floor courts protect the building from the heat. The open entrance portico leads between pylons toward winding ramps, that lead to upper floor offices. Great sculptured spaces result for the visitor.

38

39

42

43

42, 44 Ahmedabad, Shodhan House, 1951

Architect: Le Corbusier

Following the construction of Chandigarh, some industrialists in the city of Ahmedabad invited Le Corbusier to build houses and the headquarters of the Millowners organisation. The most dramatic of these is the Villa Shodhan, a 3 storey building of sculptural plasticity and penetrating spaces intertwining exteriors and interiors, with modular proportioned glass and solid infill walls.

43, 45 Ahmedabad, Sarabhai House, 1955

Architect: Le Corbusier

This ground level house is built of regular low concrete arches supported on regularly spaced beams on brick walls. The open interior in this tropical climate allows air currents across and longitudinally through the entire house. For the sons of the house a concrete slide allows their speedy descent into the swimming pool in the garden.

46

46, 47 Ahmedabad, Millowners' Association Building, 1954

Architect: Le Corbusier
Overlooking a river edge, the street approach leads over an inclined ramp into the open central space, to the offices and meeting halls. Both east and west facades are protected by brise-soleil from the strong sunlight. The form-boarded concrete gives a rugged texture to the entire structure.

48 Ahmedabad, Indian Institute of Management, 1963-74

Architect: Louis Kahn
This 65 acre campus accommodates all teaching areas, staff and student housing, in garden courts. The flat arched brick façades are tied with tensioned concrete lintels that give a distinctive form to the whole complex.

Thailand

Bangkok, the modern capital of Thailand, was founded in 1782 and consisted of encircling moats and walls which guarded the hinterland from the entrance of the main river.

King Rama V patronised European architecture and town planning which resulted in an amalgam of Victorian and Thai style structures.

The most remarkable assembly of such buildings are in the wall enclosed Grand Palace, used by the King for certain ceremonial occasions. Gold encrusted high pointed spire shrines, colourful sculptured figures and triple layered gabled religious pavilions create an astonishing group of buildings.

The tremendous reclining golden Buddha, 46 metres long and 15 metres high, is only one of 394 gilded Buddha images in temples and museums throughout Bangkok.

1-3 Bangkok, Grand Palace, 1782
The wall enclosed Grand Palace contains Bangkok's glistening golden landmark; a huge pointed spire shrine.

, 5 Bangkok, Wat Pho, 1781
his wat contains the golden reclining
uddha, it is the world's longest, 46 metres
ng.

4

5

Cambodia

During the Khmer Kingdom of Angkor from 900-1200 AD some of the world's most magnificent architectural masterpieces were constructed. The Angkor area consists of various compounds of Hindu and Buddhist structures and contain over 70 major temples and other buildings. The mostly square concentric courts contain colonnaded galleries with the focal tower buildings increasing in height at intersections.

After Siamese attacks Angkor was abandoned in the 15th Century and only Angkor Wat remained, as a shrine for Buddhist pilgrims. The other temple structures became enveloped by the tropical forest with huge trees growing out of some of the compounds, until restorations commenced in 1908.

From my observation, I believe that Angkor Wat is the only area built on a two metre thick basalt stone foundation, in comparison to other areas that have very thin and largely collapsed foundations. That is the main reason for Angkor's survival. Structural failures also occurred since only layers of progressively cantilevered stone were used across gallery roofs, since segmental arch construction was unknown at the time.

Of great interest are the "apsara, or heavenly nymph" reliefs appearing on all buildings. Bas-reliefs cover entire walls, depicting warriors in battle and marching elephants.

1 Angkor Wat, 12th Century
Entrance Gallery with carved basalt relief sculptures.

2

2 Angkor Wat
Entrance causeway with tower structures.

3, 4 Angkor Wat
Tower structure rising from courtyard and
ground plan showing central structures and
open courts.

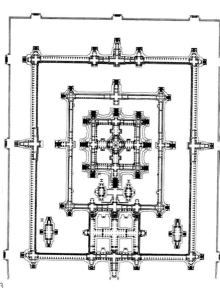

3

5

5-7 Angkor Wat

"Apsara" relief sculptures and views of courts.

8

9

8 Angkor Thom, South Gate
Main entrance gate lined with heads of gods and demons.

9 Angkor Thom, Bayon, 1200
Entry from reflecting pool.

10, 11, 13 Angkor Wat
Bas-relief wall sculptures.

12 Angkor Thom
Terrace of carved elephants.

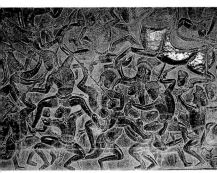

15

16

14 Angkor Thom, Bayon
One of many enigmatically smiling carved heads.

15 Angkor Thom
Centre of Royal Palace.

16 Ta Prohm, 1186
This Buddhist Temple has been left to be swallowed by the jungle, the buildings have been enveloped by tree root structures for centuries.

17

18

19

20

17-21 Banteay Srei, 10th Century
This Hindu temple is decorated with beautiful filigree carved reliefs depicting deities.

22 Preah Neak Pean, 12th Century
Standing in a large pool, is a central "island" Buddhist temple statue.

22

Australia

The establishment of a penal colony in Australia soon after the first landings in 1788 included an English architect Francis Greenway who had been transported for committing a forgery. Upon his arrival, Governor Macquarie engaged him to design numerous public buildings which became the pride of Australia's colonial architecture. The buildings were intelligently modified 18th Century English Georgian work within the restricted means available in the colony and adjusted to the semi tropical climate. With the arrival of large numbers of settlers and immigrant workers in the early 19th Century, continuous row housing or "terraces" were built. They were adapted versions of English prototypes with shaded verandahs and decorative iron railings, brought from Europe as ballast in sailing ships.

Of all the architecture produced in the intervening years only one building stands out dramatically which has become the very icon of the country; the Sydney Opera House. The 1957 international competition was won by the Danish architect Jørn Utzon. Standing on a peninsula reaching into the harbour, the multiple vaulted forms of the building are based on ingenious geometry, executed in prestressed precast concrete ribs with a white glazed exterior surface. Following a 1966 change in Government, and the building structurally complete, Jørn Utzon was dismissed and left the country never to return. His estimate of time to complete the building had been considered excessive at one and a half years. It took the new government seven years to complete the work in 1973, with a resulting interior, universally considered to be a great disappointment.

Australia's record in treating architects is very poor. Walter Burley Griffin, the Chicago architect who won the international competition for the design of the country's capital Canberra, never built there and left the country. The moral rights and freedom of architectural endeavour is discouraging with aesthetic jurisdiction remaining in the hand of untrained local government bureaucrats.

2

1 Sydney, Hyde Park Barracks, 1817-19
Architect: Francis Greenway
A typical colonial brick building of fine proportions following English Georgian precedence.

2 Sydney, Terrace House, mid 19th Century
Typical row house with shaded verandah and English iron railings imported as ballast on sailing ships.

3 Francis Greenway, 1777-1837

4

4 Sydney, Elizabeth Bay House, 1835
Architect: John Verge
Elegant house interior space reflecting English Georgian taste.

5 Sydney, The Mint, 1814
Typical colonial era building with colonnaded verandahs.

6 Sydney, Terrace Houses, late 19th Century
Typical stepping up continuous terrace row houses representative of hilly inner districts of the city. Brick cross walls support timber floors and slate roofs. The narrow allotments have private enclosed rear gardens.

7 Sydney, Opera House, 1957-73
Architect: Jørn Utzon
Selected at an international architectural competition, this unique precast concrete ribbed structure is covered with glazed white tiles. After structural completion, there was a dispute between Utzon and the newly elected state government client, following which the architect was dismissed in 1966, never to return. The building was completed by others and resulted in disappointing interiors. The exterior Opera House design is considered the very icon of Australia.

Biography

Harry Seidler 1923-2006 who was born in Vienna Austria, became Australia's foremost architect.

Following the anschluss occupation in 1938 he fled to England where, after the outbreak of war in 1940, he was interned as an enemy alien. During his internment he was transported to Quebec Canada, and almost two years later he was released to study architecture at the University of Manitoba.

In 1945-46 he attended the Master's class at Harvard University as a student of Walter Gropius. He later studied design under Josef Albers at Black Mountain College.

He worked with Marcel Breuer in New York (1946-48) and with Oscar Niemeyer in Brazil on his way to Australia in 1948.

He went to Australia to build a house for his parents; the 'Rose Seidler House' in Sydney 1950, which is now a house museum owned and operated by the Historic Houses Trust of NSW.

During over fifty years of practice he built a great variety of work from houses to skyscrapers, both in Australian cities and internationally. His work is widely published and he won many awards including the RIBA Gold Medal in 1996. He has taught and lectured extensively. One of his last works included a housing community beside the Danube in Vienna.

During his many travels to his various international projects, Seidler developed a love of photography to document what he considered to be the peak achievements of architecture throughout the ages.

This is the first book of his photography. Seidler's work is not illustrated in this book. For a pictorial record of the architectural work of Harry Seidler and Associates see www.seidler.net.au.